How do I know I'm doing right?

Revised Edition

How do I know
I'm doing right?

Toward the Formation
of a Christian Conscience

GERARD S. SLOYAN

Mary Perkins Ryan, General Editor

Sponsored by the
National Center of Religious Education—CCD,
Washington, D.C.

 Pflaum

Nihil Obstat:
Rev. Walter J. Schmitz, S.T.D.
Censor Deputatus

Imprimatur:
Most Rev. William W. Baum, D.D., S.T.D.
Archbishop of Washington
April 26, 1976

ISBN: 0-8278-2132-8
Library of Congress Catalog Card Number: 67-19685

Contents

CHAPTER 1

Changing Church, Changing Society

Do not think that I have come to abolish the law and the prophets. I have come, not to abolish them, but to fulfill them. Of this much I assure you: until heaven and earth pass away, not the smallest letter of the law, not the smallest part of a letter, shall be done away with until it all comes true . . . I tell you, unless your holiness surpasses that of the scribes and Pharisees, you shall not enter the kingdom of God . . . Say "Yes" when you mean "Yes" and "No" when you mean "No." Anything beyond that is from the evil one.

Matthew 5:17f.; 20; 37

Is it important to do what is right in life? Is there such a thing as an "ethical imperative," a line of human behavior that has about it a certain "oughtness"? If so, who is to decide ultimately what ought to be done? Is it God, acting as our infallible teacher? Is it the sages of the centuries, the great ethical guides such as Confucius and Socrates and Jesus (the latter understood by many not to speak with God's voice) and Aquinas and Kant? Or does man simply know from his own nature how he should act? Who will guide us in what to do, and what to do in the specific choices we are faced with? Is there any human teacher

1

to convict us of sin or to assure us that we are traveling the path of virtue—taken here as ordinary human goodness?

Unless we can find some answers to these questions, many of us who are Christians from birth or by family tradition will continue to be uncertain in matters where we once felt fully assured.

Perhaps it is an exaggeration to speak of widespread insecurity among Christians over moral choices. It may be that things are much more stable than they appear, or that they are quite as they always were. The posture taken above may be unduly alarmist. Yet it hardly seems so when one moves about the country and talks with many and different kinds of people. There appears to be a growing uncertainty about what things are right and wrong to do. Conscientious parents are the ones who suffer most from this climate. They say that they need more help, more guidance than there is available to them.

The conviction in possession, so to say, is that there was a body of teaching on human behavior among the Israelites of old that was stated summarily under ten major headings or commandments, and that Jesus of Nazareth assumed that this teaching had come through Moses from the one he called his heavenly Father. He disagreed strongly with some of the rabbinic moral teaching current in his day, but with the central core of ethical teaching presented in the books of Exodus, Deuteronomy, and the prophets, and the interpretation given it by many rabbinic teachers, he did not differ. What we have from Jesus is the reminder that human customs and religious folkways can never acquire the force of divine law that attaches to the prohibition against murder or false witness. He also stressed certain refinements of the Mosaic teaching, notably, the possibility of sinning in one's heart by intention. He was by no means alone among Jewish teachers in this, but he did it so consistently that he is rightly connected with the notion of the "interiorization" of commands and precepts received—not as the initiator of the idea but as one of the great Jewish moralists who stressed it.

Overall, Jesus is known to the Christian as a "teacher sent by God" (John 3:2) as Moses was, but at the same time one who altered Jewish ethical teaching in a few important particulars. His prohibition of remarriage after divorce is one such case (Luke 16:18). The high value he apparently put on the unmarried life for cause is another (Matthew 19:12). After that, we have a great number of moral specifics that flow from Jesus' spirit if not from the letter of his words. Among the results of his teaching are a certain slow diminishment of the institution of slavery, the conviction of some of his followers that war as a way of settling political differences is totally incompatible with his spirit, the strong contemporary feeling in certain Christian circles against capital punishment, and the slow but growing decline of male dominance over females. In general, Jesus' way is the way of mercy and peace, not of vengefulness and strife. Yet it well may be asked why his merciful and peaceful stance has had such little practical effect among those who hail him as their teacher.

The seeds of his doctrine were already richly sown in Israelite teaching. Jesus, whom Christians venerate as "the Lord," simply brought many of these green shoots to the surface. At the hands of Jewish and Christian teachers since his day—which was the lifetime directly after that of the gentle rabbi Hillel— the Mosaic seeds have been coming to fruition in the two religious traditions.

For Christians, the authentic interpreter of Jesus

since the day of his glorification as Lord and Christ has been the Holy Spirit. This Advocate whom he sent from the Father dwells in the midst of the community (what came to be known as "the church") wherever it is realized. The Paraclete (an Anglicization of the Greek word used in the fourth Gospel) abides in the heart of anyone who receives him. It is not an easy matter, however, for individuals or for the whole assembly of believers to recognize the Spirit's voice. Leaving oneself open to his influence is of paramount importance.

A second element in Christians' ideas about "rightness" is the reality of conscience—actually, another word for "consciousness"—which is self-awareness with respect to right- and wrongdoing. The formation of conscience should never take place for the Christian apart from the action of the Spirit, brought on at times by active consultation of him.

Another factor is moral consensus: the conviction on the part of Christians as Christians, or of people of good will generally, that a certain line of behavior is here and now morally acceptable or reprehensible, viz., that something is right in these circumstances and perhaps a necessay course of action or, conversely, that it is not right in these circumstances and may not be done, perhaps in any circumstances.

Again, for the Christian in the Roman Catholic tradition, just as for the Protestant and the Jew, the inspired word of Scripture is an important norm in determining what one's behavior shall be. But Catholics only recently have come to know biblical teaching at first hand on any large scale. Numbers of them have become regular Bible readers only in the last few decades. For the many Catholics who never consult the prophets, the evangelists, or St. Paul, Christian moral teaching is something that comes through ordinary pulpit preaching, through the positions their bishops take on public and private morality, and through the Pope when he declares himself on issues like marriage, genocide, or war.

In general, Catholics do not make distinctions among their various moral teachers, whether they be Jesus or Paul, pope, bishops, or priests. They tend to spead of "what the church teaches," and they have her moral teaching pretty straight. They may not like all that the church teaches, or even abide by certain parts of it; but in the area of knowledge, they are aware generally of what is approved and disapproved by the church when it acts as a teacher.

The question for some is: Has the church itself got moral teaching straight? For the most part, the church has been a good guide—even if one not entirely free from ambivalence in its teaching of morality. This derives from the kind of institution the church is. To say that there is some ambivalence in its teaching is not to say anything about the Holy Spirit's deserting the church, but a good deal about its members' not being faithful to him. Because of certain ambiguities in the church's moral teaching, the result of infidelities large and small, it is not surprising that the faithful who make up that church—clergy and laity alike—are experiencing uncertainties in the present age.

One matter that requires serious discussion is the fact that the most flagrant offenses against faith and charity and breaches of church discipline both have carried with them the description, "serious sin." A man who hates his brother-in-law with a gnawing hatred and a woman who absents herself from Mass on Sunday are not, one presumes, in the same condition of soul. Yet the two infractions have been classified similarly for purposes of the contrition that should be expressed. Both matters are called "grave sin."

5

The further sobering fact is that an overt act of omission is more readily catalogued as "a sin" than a continuing, unrepentant state of heart. A Catholic under the catechetical conditions of the last few centuries could readily come to identify Mass-missing as his greater offense and corrosive domestic discord as his lesser.

Needless to say, a confusion such as this is very unhealthy for anyone's moral life. It is potentially destructive of all clear vision. Yet many patterns of moral education continue forcefully to uphold it. No infractions of church law is on a par with failure in "mercy, justice, and good faith"—for Jesus "the weightier matters of the law" (Matthew 23:23). Yet this priority has not been reflected in ordinary moral education or in the speech habits of Catholics when they discuss these questions.

The church, needless to say, is free to establish rules and regulations for persons in the religious state. Laws regulating marriage and interfaith worship likewise are helpful and at times necessary. None of these regulations, however, is to be conceived in exactly the same terms as the heartland of the Christian ethos, which is love.

When an infraction of church discipline is described as mortally sinful it can be such because it is rooted in contempt for God—though one does not need church law to make a sin of that—or because it comprises a scandal to the onlooker. Either of the two would be a sin against love. But the breaking of a church-made rule cannot fall into the category of serious sin *in itself*. It is always a failure in love under some other heading. Because this important distinction is frequently not made, even by those who are "teachers in Israel," Catholics find themselves needlessly in false states of conscience. Under such handicaps of education, any commitment to a way of perfection—and Christian love unquestionably is that—is likely to be accompanied by the counterfeit state of perfection that consists of fulfilling a code of the most exacting sort. Yet code morality is the very antithesis of the teaching of Jesus.

The fact that code morality is put forward as if it had the full sanction of Jesus is the chief ambivalence of moral teaching as it has been proposed in the Catholic church.

Another puzzling confusion for Catholics (i.e., beyond that caused by church laws seeming to bind with equal gravity as the law of the Gospel) is the fact that the moral requirement in certain important matters seems to be undergoing change. Up until quite recently, the church never taught that a white person had to respect Blacks or Chicanos or Puerto Ricans or care to have them as neighbors or social companions. Now a Catholic reads in a bishop's pastoral letter that opposition to open housing or integrated schooling can be gravely sinful. Ten and fifteen years ago, a couple with a large and growing family was led unequivocally to believe that any single thing they did to interfere with conception by artificial means (i.e. anything but the rhythm method) would merit eternal condemnation for them. The Pope and many bishops are still saying that. At the same time, the Pope and all the bishops failed to say it unequivocally at Vatican Council II. Rather, the teaching there was that parents must bring children into the world "with human and Christian responsibility" *(Constitution on the Church Today)*. The document adds: "The parents themselves should ultimately make this judgment in the sight of God. But in their manner of acting, spouses should be aware that they cannot act arbitrarily. They must always be governed by a conscience conformed to the divine law

7

itself and should be submissive toward the Church's teaching office . . ." It is not secret that many bishops and some national hierarchies around the world have fallen silent on the Pope's teaching on contraception as if it were the only position held by the church's teaching office, while stressing the Council's teachings with its latitude for parental judgment in God's sight.

Or, take a matter in a less important sphere than new human life or respect for human persons: up until a few decades ago, it was clear beyond discussion that in our culture it was immodest for women to expose their breasts; now it seems that in certain circumstances the bosom can and will be open to view—in media like the films or in real life—without sin or shame. The possibility of immodesty continues, of course, but the line is no longer firm, the question no longer absolute.

To sum up, Christians were always familiar with the moral axiom, "Circumstances alter cases"; but they are now uncertain on a large scale as to what are the circumstances and which the cases. Putting it bluntly, they ask: "Is everything relative? What has happened to the church as a moral teacher? Where is it all going to end?"

Today's moral confusion is by no means a phenomenon confined to Catholics, since all humanity alike is burdened with decisions over sex, ethnicity, money, and property. Generally speaking, people are capable of moral indignation at the unspeakable horror of the destruction by Hitler of six million Jews. Yet the prospect of living in a neighborhood or a resort area where no Jews are allowed attracts many of the same people instead of filling them with loathing and disgust. The German happening and the American happening are very closely allied—namely, seeing to it that certain people as a class shall be nonexistent in the lives of others—yet the affinity of the two evils is to many not immediately apparent.

Or take misconduct in public office in the larger context of business ethics. When an elected official fails to report large sums that come to him through the influence he exercises in office—usually to avoid the detection that declaring the income would bring—the public conscience is affronted as soon as the tax-evasion story hits the papers. Yet not everyone is indignant. Some say cynically: "They all do it. He just got caught." Not a few who deplore the scandal—in car pools, at public bars, or on commuter trains—are compromising themselves similarly on a smaller scale. Indeed, so high is the tolerance for private gain from public office that one must conclude that millions of Americans hesitate to speak out against it because they themselves harbor an unexpressed approval of the practice.

The general sentiment with regard to sexual promiscuity in our culture continues to be a contemptuous: "He's a tomcat" or "She's a tramp." Yet infractions of marital fidelity on a smaller scale are commonplace. People have "affairs," which are crowned with a kind of respectability: "I'm divorcing my wife, you know. I don't suppose I'll marry right away, but I won't rule it out. Well, yes, as a matter of fact, there is someone I've been seeing a good deal of." With respect to young people and premarital sex experience, Margaret Mead observes that the prevailing parental caution is, "Don't get pregnant, but if you do we'll give you a nice church wedding."

The above illustrations taken at random are meant to point up what everyone realizes: that there are behavior patterns that cause uneasiness when they reach a certain magnitude; but short of an incident (i.e., getting caught), they are attended by a high individual and social tolerance. In a word, our culture lives a double standard. People living in a culture such as ours can hardly help suffering from confusion about many moral questions, since a consensus on morality no longer exists. In many areas of behavior, our society no longer agrees generally that a certain thing is right or wrong. Many things are considered sectarian matters, e.g., gambling is a sin for some Protestants, abortion is a sin for Catholics. Many Catholics who formerly felt sure that "what the church teaches" must be an infallible guide to right behavior are wondering now—particularly since the silences and the thunders that have followed Vatican II—how this teaching can be infallible, or what infallibility means when one hears no teaching on grave matters. It now appears that moral teaching in the past not only overemphasized obedience to church-made rules and underemphasized Christ's law of love, but that it has undergone modification on substantive matters. Most important of all, it has grown pusillanimous on matters of great moment while concentrating heavily on a limited range of problems.

Perhaps one cause of the present confusion is that many Catholics have taken passive acceptance of what the church teaches or fails to teach in moral matters as a substitute for forming their own consciences. But forming their own consciences is something they must do according to the teaching of Jesus, as it is interpreted by the Spirit dwelling in the church. The process of forming a Christian conscience should be for each of us a lifelong search to discover what God is asking of us in concrete situations. We have tended unfortunately to reduce it to remembering what we learned in religion classes. Another pattern, fading fast, was to consult a priest on what we should do in a given situation. "The church," in such an approach to morality, always was understood to mean other people in the church and specifically the clergy. Perhaps most commonly of all nowadays is that many Catholics, having set the moral teaching of the church behind them, have set all moral teaching behind them. Such solutions can never be satisfactory. Many areas of conduct have not yet been explored sufficiently by moral theology—race-relations, for example, homosexual attraction, the right to die. Even if they could be, each concrete situation is in some way unique, and rules cannot be made to fit this uniqueness. More important, the whole bearing of the teaching of Jesus is that blind obedience to detailed precepts is not what God wants. God asks for a free and loving response. This means that we have to start asking ourselves in all matters: What is the loving thing to do in this situation?

In other words, we have to work within a believing church to form a Christian conscience.

But to point out the necessity of forming a Christian conscience brings up a further source of confusion for Catholics. When people start "following their consciences" rather than simply doing what others in the church tell them to do, aren't they heading for trouble? Are they not called simply to be obedient to the teachers in the church if they have freely accepted life in the church as their means of obedience to Christ? We will discuss this question and some of its implications in the following chapter.

DISCUSSION QUESTIONS

Do you think that there is more uncertainty among Catholics today than there was ten or twenty years ago over what is right or wrong, and over the role of the church as their teacher in these matters? Might such uncertainty have some good effects in the long run? If so, how?

Does the idea worry you that "the teaching of the church," as you have received it and understand it, may have been affected by variable human factors past and present, even though the church has Christ's promise that the Holy Spirit will never desert it? How do you understand the presence of the Spirit in the church, and the nature of the church as a "pilgrim" as explained in the *Constitution on the Church* of Vatican Council II?

What could be done effectively to convince adult Catholics that all forms of ethnic and racial discrimination are sinful, even though they were not taught so as children?

Do most Catholics think of the formation of their conscience as an on-going process for which they are responsible and for which they need the help of the Holy Spirit? Would the spread of such a conviction make a difference in the general tone of Catholic life? How?

The mouth of the just man tells of wisdom
  and his tongue utters what is right.
The law of his God is in his heart,
  and his steps do not falter.

Psalm 37:30-31

CHAPTER 2

Obedience and Conscience

"When all these things which I have set before you, the things blessed and the things cursed, are fulfilled in you . . . and . . . you ponder them in your heart: . . . then provided that you and your children return to the Lord, your God, and heed his voice with all your heart and all your soul, just as I now command you, the Lord, your God, will change your lot . . . (He) will again take delight in your prosperity, even as he took delight in your fathers', if only you heed the voice of the Lord, your God, and keep his commandments and statutes . . . with all your heart and all your soul . . . For this command which I enjoin on you today is not too mysterious and remote for you. It is not up in the sky, that you should say, 'Who will go up in the sky to get it for us and tell us of it, that we may carry it out?' Nor is it across the sea, that you should say, 'Who will cross the sea to get it for us and tell us of it, that we may carry it out?' No, it is something very near to you, already in your mouths and in your hearts; you have only to carry it out."

Deuteronomy 30:1-3; 9; 11-14

Two things should be clear from the discussion thus far. One is that whereas moral teaching for which divine sanction is claimed may at times take the form,

"This is forbidden" or "That is obligatory," what is really being said is—with God himself as the speaker: "Decide freely on the basis of prudent judgment what you will do in these circumstances." Obedience to God is a matter of love, and love is not forced. The second thing that emerges is that if people are required to determine their own course of action, they need help in making right choices. (We do not speak of God's grace here; this we assume.) People cannot bear the heavy burden of choosing on their own, isolated from the experience of others who have been in similar situations. Freedom is the greatest human good; but in holding onto this precious treasure, we need all the human help we can get to bear the weight of continual free choice. As the limits of external freedom expand, people tend either to lead libertarian lives beholden to no one or else to be terrified by all the choices that lie open before them. They will be immobilized in the second case, making none of the possible choices in an effective way, because the structures they need in which to make them do not exist.

The previous chapter mentioned "code morality" in a way that clearly put it in second place to a scheme of deliberate choices made by the individual from within, based on justice and love. This apparent putting in opposition of a code ethic and a love ethic will help to underline a difficulty that many Christians are experiencing. They express themselves this way: "God made man, didn't he? Surely he has the right to command him as to how he ought to act. That's the meaning of the 'ten commandments,' isn't it, God telling man how to act? And doesn't the same thing hold true from the time God became man and founded the church? What kind of church would it be if God couldn't use it to command us about the way he wants us to serve him?''

As this outlook is expressed, it seems to be the best possible view of God's sovereign rights over his creatures. A greater docility or openness to the divine command is hard to conceive. Yet what it may reflect in fact is the temperament or disposition of the speaker rather than any profound Christian conviction. A person who poses the question in this way may be someone who by nature wants to be led. Decision-making puts such a person ill at ease. Religion and its attendant morality is for that person essentially a heteronomous affair. That means that the law *(nómos)* of human behavior has to come from another *(héteros);* it cannot originate within the self *(autós).*

The mention of autonomous or inner-originating human conduct causes panic in certain hearts. Such persons have the convenient device available of being able to claim the highest docility to the divine command. They resent it bitterly when it is pointed out to them that God does not deal with human beings in this way. He respects human nature so fully that he is not pleased with our choices until we interiorize them. He wants us to grasp the way in which a right course of action is a demand of our humanity, and one that we ourselves come to see as right. It is virtuous to follow a divine command only when a person realizes, even though imperfectly, the fittingness of this obedience as a mode of response for the individual. Blind obedience may have something to recommend it at a fire, but in ordinary circumstances it is inhuman and unworthy of our consideration. God does not wish from us in any circumstances the behavior expected of an automaton or a slave.

The idea is strongly entrenched, however, that God or the church must tell us what to do. Many men in holy orders have had this notion, especially with respect to the church as a teacher. They have been succeeded lately by a highly verbal segment of the laity that holds the same position. Both obviously are of the other-directed temperament. It is important to keep in mind that such persons may or may not be distinguished by their obedience to God. The point is that every Christian who cries "Obedience!" and decries "Disobedience!" must subject himself to scrutiny to see how interested he is in this lofty virtue and its opposite vice. And we must subject each other to such scrutiny in a spirit of hard-headed mutual respect. Proponents of an attitude of docility may simply have hit upon aura-invested watchwords as a cloak for their fear of responsible choice.

Allied to the question of God (or Christ or the church) as the teacher of humanity through clear commands is that of how much we are left on our own as Christians to determine our course of action. The old norm—serviceable enough, or so it seemed—was that one had to obey one's parents or husband or wife or religious superior or bishop in everything "except a sinful command" or when some other course of action was clearly indicated by our neighbor's need. Nowadays, however, adolescents claim a maturity by which they consider themselves absolved from conforming to the commands of their parents. They do not do as they are told, and they do not consider the infraction disobedience. It is rather their "mature response in their situation." Such is the common case in family homes and high schools and colleges.

The cases of claims for the autonomy of conscience that come to public notice—of Catholic people, at least—occur chiefly in the ranks of the clergy. A bishop will tell a priest that he may not speak publicly on specific means to relieve the needs of the poor in the city where he serves, or that he may not run for public office. The priest will say that he is sympathetic to his bishop's wish but that he cannot in conscience keep silent or fail to take effective steps to meet certain social abuses head on. The bishop's command may be described by the priest as based on such an incomplete grasp of the total situation that it cannot be considered binding. In other words, the claim is made for the demands of individual conscience over the command of a superior: "We must obey God rather than men," in St. Peter's ringing phrase (Acts 5:30). Some of these situations end in a bishop's suspending a priest from any exercise of his office. The priest, meanwhile, may continue to celebrate Mass because he feels in conscience that the suspension doesn't bind him. Or he may resign from the priesthood because he feels he cannot do a priest's work.

A similar case of long standing is that of the Catholic man or woman who takes a second marriage partner while the first one still lives. "We wrestled with this problem," the new couple says, "and we concluded that it was the right thing to do. We have no quarrel with the church's legislation. In fact, we're against divorce ourselves. It just seemed that in this case we were doing what was right. We know the Lord will understand, even though the church doesn't." Catholic priests who marry, as some tens of thousands have done in the last decade, often make a similar claim for the supremacy of conscience: "We had to make a mature decision in faith. We have no consciousness of wrongdoing, only a feeling of liberation. It's one of those matters where the church's law will have to catch up with practice. The church's authorities intimated at every turn that we did wrong, but we are a part of that church, and we know we did right."

Lay people, seeing such a forthright expression of the autonomy of individual conscience attributed to a priest, react in either of several ways. They are scandalized at the position taken and say it is no wonder ordinary people are confused; they affect to be scandalized because it suits their posture to do so; or they observe that it is about time that the hypocrisy in the church ended and that everyone admitted that a person looks for relief when the shoe pinches, no matter what his state. The latter group tends to think that clerical morality is catching up with lay morality, and none too soon at that. A fourth reaction, more thoughtful than any of the above, is to ask about the wisdom of the church's putting on the defensive those who follow their consciences in making a serious decision about vocation.

Meanwhile, the Christian's case for following his conscience as the safest, surest norm in moral matters has been obscured: first, perhaps, by the way certain claimants have had recourse to the norm, then by the unqualified resistance to their claim by those who accuse them of old-style, wilful selfishness. Yet it is our Christian duty to form our consciences and to follow them. It is also our duty to support and not to speak ill of those who by their own declaration are following their consciences.

Here is a mixed bag of questions to which no ready answer is available:

If a citizen has no confidence in the rightness of a war-action the country is engaged in, is it right for that person to do everything in his or her power to publicize, disrupt, or fail to cooperate in the effort, including going to another country and expecting amnesty afterward? Why are the German citizens of thirty and forty years ago held accountable for their silence while modern populations do not seem to be?

At what point should an office-holder in a democracy be brought to trial, nationally or internationally, when his public policy decisions affect the welfare of millions adversely?

What motivations to chastity can parents or teachers hold out to youth when the likelihood of pregnancy or venereal disease, the two greatest practical deterrents up till now, are reduced to near zero point? "It's sinful" or "Christians don't do that" rings hollow unless adults can provide youth—and one another—with convincing reasons why it is wrong, why chastity may not be redefined to include sexual experience apart from marriage, in light of our altered physiological and psychological knowledge. Why, precisely, is it wrong to be unchaste?

In being sensitive to the demands of charity in speech, when must one be silent? When may one speak? When must one speak? Why, in a word, is Jesus' warning against casting the first stone (John 8:7) so popular when one group disapproves another?

What must the position of the world community be on the impending births of millions for whom it is clear—not hypothetical—that there will not be enough food?

May an individual approach the Eucharist freely without confessing sin when she or he is struggling hard to terminate a habit of sexual self-excitation?

Does not the same need for the Lord's Body on a regular basis extend to an engaged couple in their daily struggle to be chaste, marked as they are by regression as well as progress?

How can the state require the registration of motor vehicles but not of firearms? Permit the sale of alcohol but not of marijuana?

How can a government in justice tolerate segregation or exclusivism of any sort in patterns of housing? In employment? In schools? How can it enforce a

19

move from adequate to inferior schooling for some while trying to achieve adequate schooling for others?

This small book would be seriously unfair to the reader if it gave the impression that it could provide a solution to all these problems. It can do a few important things, however. It can identify some of the questions in moral matters that need asking and help its readers get launched on a mature discussion of them. It can convey the urgency of a public morality, without which a private morality is almost impossible for individuals. It can touch on the basic question of whether there is such a thing as an absolute in moral matters (such as God's will that certain actions be avoided always and in every circumstance), or whether, given that fact of God's will to goodness, morality is relative (situational, contextual) by its very nature. It can ask whether the naming of moral "absolutes" is included in that preferring of the Sabbath to man, which Jesus warned against so sternly. It can speak of the force of the "natural law," that concept which the Catholic-college educated person of thirty or older seems to be so committed to (or rebelliously angry against) and which other informed adults seem not to have heard of.

These pages can speak of what the human person should be as the best guide to the rightness of his or her choices. They also can ask whether the individual who was called at Baptism to be new in Christ has any course of action but to search for completeness as a human being. In other words, is the ethical way of the Christian simply identical with the way of humanity at its best? What difference is there, if any, between Christian morality and human morality? Are there sins for Catholics that are not sins for other people?

Lastly, these pages can ask whether it is God the Father who is the supreme arbiter of rightdoing in human life, or Jesus the Lord, or the Holy Spirit. Is the last court of human appeal the law implanted in the human heart or the human person as God reveals him to himself? Or, if these questions as posed are false ones, what must their true wording be?

DISCUSSION QUESTIONS

How can God give the human race commandments and at the same time want only free, deliberate choices in response and not mere conformity to commandments?

It seems to be agreed generally that Catholic religious education in the past tended to foster the idea of moral conduct as consisting primarily in obedience rather than personal responsibility for decisions. What might have been some of the reasons (social, ethnic, historical, etc.) for this tendency? Why might a change be needed today?

In what sense would you say that individual conscience is supreme, and in what sense not supreme?

Must a person have a sufficient reason for every moral choice he or she makes? Are there not some cases where, not knowing reasons in their fullness, a person is justified nonetheless in doing as the church teaches simply because the church so teaches?

How is it that the easiest argument to get started in Catholic circles is whether morality is objective or subjective, absolute or relative? Why cannot an intelligent argument be launched on this subject until a few terms are carefully defined?

That is not what you learned when you learned Christ! I am supposing, of course, that he has been preached and taught to you in accord with the truth that is in Jesus: namely, that you must lay aside your former way of life and old self which deteriorates through illusion and desire, and acquire a fresh, spiritual way of thinking. You must put on that new man created in God's image, whose justice and holiness are born of truth.

See to it, then, that you put an end to lying; let everyone speak the truth to his neighbor, for we are members of one another. If you are angry, let it be without sin. The sun must not go down on your wrath . . . Get rid of all bitterness, all passion and anger, harsh words, slander, and malice of every kind. In place of these, be kind to one another, compassionate, and mutually forgiving, just as God has forgiven you in Christ.

Be imitators of God as his dear children. Follow the way of love, even as Christ loved you. . . .

There was a time when you were in darkness, but now you are light in the Lord. Well, then, live as children of light. . . . Be correct in your judgment of what pleases the Lord. . . .

Keep careful watch over your conduct. Do not act like fools, but like those who are thoughtful. . . . Defer to one another out of reverence for Christ.

Ephesians 4:20-26; 31-32; 5:1-2a; 8; 10; 15; 21

CHAPTER 3

The Bible as Source

Woe to him who builds his house on wrong,
*   his terraces on injustice;*
Who works his neighbor without pay,
*   and gives him no wages. . . .*
Must you prove your rank among kings
*   by competing with them in cedar?*
Did not your father eat and drink?
*   He did what was right and just,*
*   and it went well with him.*
Because he dispensed justice to the weak and poor,
*   it went well with him.*
Is this not true knowledge of me?
*   says the Lord.*
But your eyes and heart are set on nothing
*   except on your own gain,*
On shedding innocent blood,
*   on practicing oppression and extortion.*

Jeremiah 22:13; 15ff.

The wrath of God is being revealed from heaven
against the irreligious and perverse spirit of men who,
in this perversity of theirs, hinder the truth. In fact,
whatever can be known about God is clear to them; he
himself made it so. Since the creation of the world,
invisible realities, God's eternal power and divinity,

*have become visible, recognized through the things he
has made. Therefore these men are inexcusable. They
certainly had knowledge of God, yet they did not
glorify him as God or give him thanks; they stultified
themselves through speculating to no purpose, and
their senseless hearts were darkened. They claimed to
be wise, but turned into fools instead. . . . They did
not see fit to acknowledge God, so God delivered
them up to their own depraved sense to do what is
unseemly. . . . They know God's just decree that all
who do such things deserve death; yet they not only do
them but approve them in others.*

Romans 1:18-22; 28; 32

In the last two chapters, we have been raising problems and asking questions. We have not attempted to
solve any, certainly not by the way we framed the
questions for discussion.

A discussion of moral or ethical conduct can begin
logically at any number of places. Human nature is a
starting-point for the philosophically inclined, though
they are not too many. The human situation in life, the
setting in which people find themselves, is probably
the universal starting-point. That and the religious
heritage they have received.

We are going to assume that, for readers of this
book, moral life has something to do with religion.
Such readers may not be clear whether they are ethical
because they are Christian (or Jewish or Muslim), or
Christian (or Jewish or Muslim) because they are
ethical—or whether the two, namely being religious
and being ethical—are identical. They do know, however, that for them the notions of religion and conduct
are intimately related. They are prepared to discuss
human behavior in a context of religious faith.

Many people in the Western world, it seems, have a high ethical standard and no particular religious commitment. Religious persons, especially Christians, like to deny this possibility; but the psychologists and the sociologists can upset them with their findings every time. The Christian moralist is often thrown back on the necessity of equating a high ethical standard with the *fullness* of Christian life to make his point. But he need not set the standard so high. The fact remains that many who do not practice or do not believe in any religion are good men and women.

Conversely, there are some people on the face of the earth who are religious but not moral and who see no contradiction in this position, and there are many who are both religious and moral but who do not consciously relate the two. They are found among those who faithfully go to temple or shrine, perform the prescribed rites and prayers, and hope to be on good terms with their gods or spirits or with the world Spirit. Questions like the morality of lying and stealing are for them (and for their religious traditions) in another department of human behavior.

The proprietress of a bordello who lights candles to our Lady so that the police won't bother her girls, or the vestryman of a church who accepts large political "gifts" acts inconsistently. The difference in these cases is that for the Christian, and equally for the Jew and the Muslim, morality is part of the warp and the woof of the worship of God. In these three traditions, the ethical and the public-prayer (and public-profession) lives of people are intertwined. The one is unthinkable without the other. That is because the God of these monotheist traditions has always been conceived as having an ethical concern. Justice in interpersonal behavior is essential to pleasing him, to doing his will.

There are ways of human life followed by still other millions that comprise an ethos or morality rather than a religion understood as the worship of God or gods. The teachings of Confucius, the Hindu and Buddhist scriptures are in this category. Each is an approach to life, a style of life, a search for harmony in life. It can be followed either with or without reference to God, Brahman, heaven, or the gods. In all of these cases—and they are not being lumped together indiscriminately here—there are important differences from Christianity, Judaism, and Islam on the nature of deity, on the nature of human freedom, and on fate or providence which suggest that in them the ethical-religious relation be treated on different terms than in the Jewish-Christian-Muslim traditions.

The latter three, even though they may experience important differences among themselves on certain questions (e.g., polygamy, marriage after divorce, reprisal for injustice), are in general of one mind on the great problems of behavior. They share a central tradition on the meaning and importance of human life. Together, they hold food and drink and sex and marriage to be unequivocally good. For the Christian, the Jew, or the Muslim, unlike the Gnostic, the Platonist, or the Hindu or Buddhist, matter is of the reality, the stuff of life; it is not an imprisonment or a decline from reality—reality being conceived as soul or spirit. On property and possession, work, war and peace, the importance of the individual, of the old and the disadvantaged, of children, even of animals, the Jew, the Christian, and the Muslim think alike.

Most importantly, they are largely at one on the key matter of how a sovereignly free God and his free creature man are partners in the business of human life. This is not to claim that their vision of the cosmos is superior. It is to say that they view man and the world differently from the Far East.

The Bible, like the Qur'an, is a religious book. It is also a book that reflects on every page a vision of human behavior. Man is called to be holy because the God who made him is holy. "Holiness," or the quality of being godlike, is seen to consist of separateness, but also of justice, mercy, and concern to an eminent degree. The prime motivation for holy behavior by mankind is free choice by God; its chief concomitant is worship, praise of his holy name.

Biblical man is invited ultimately—though this was not true in the early biblical period—to be monogamous and conjugally faithful. In the Jewish Scriptures, alleviations of this general scheme are legislated for, with respect to the male, by the institution of concubinage or minor wives. If a man deflowers a virgin, he must in justice to her father or older brother or owner marry her, or make some otherwise just indemnification. The institution of slavery is not challenged in either Testament of the Bible, but it is carefully and humanely regulated in the Mosaic books. St. Paul asked Philemon, a Christian slave-owner, to take back his runaway slave Onesimus, who had become a Christian, to "possess him forever, no longer as a slave but . . . as a beloved brother."

What seem to the modern ear harsh moral settlements in the law of Moses are in fact notable modifications of prevailing practice in the ancient Near East. Thus the famous "law of talion" (retaliation, punishment in kind; see Exodus 21:23-24) requires that if an eye is gouged out, no more than an eye be destroyed in return. It is a bloody code; but in its demand for strict justice, the net effect in that far-off time was clemency. Massive reprisals were sternly ruled out. In the moral order, this was a step forward comparable to the discovery of fire or the invention of the wheel. It no longer looks very enlightened, as practiced by both parties in the Middle East.

Israelite morality, indeed, was marked by a double standard in a way common to the whole ancient world. There was one acceptable mode of behavior toward the fellow-circumcised and another toward *ha goyim*, "the nations." The "neighbor" of Leviticus *(real)* 19:18, whom the member of the holy people had to love as himself was, understood to be a person of the same ethnic stock. At the same time, a policy of mildness in the ancient world was proposed for "the alien *(ger)* dwelling in your midst" (Leviticus 19:33).

We would be quite wrong to look down on the codified character of Mosaic morality. Such was the convention of ancient times. Israel should not be expected to have had different cultural institutions from its neighbors. What it had was a different conception of God, and this was quite enough. Israel was made in his image, not he in hers. All the many prescriptions in the law of Moses, while they spoke of a sovereign will imposed from without, added up to something quite different. This Torah or holy instruction was the way a son or daughter of the covenant should follow. The Jew should act no differently than his or her God, who was conceived of as someone dwelling at the pinnacle of ethical behavior. The difference between man and God was that God was faithful to himself and hence was always holy with respect to man, whereas man did not fulfill his calling from his God, the Lord. He fell short of his possibilities. He was not holy with respect to God, though he was called to be. This recurrent failure, amounting to rebellion, the Bible calls "sin."

It is impossible to come to terms with biblical morality apart from the notion of sin. In its earlier occurrences, the term is used indiscriminately to describe offenses against social or tribal life, against an individual, against any person, place or ordinance sacred to the Lord. This concept of "tabu" is an extremely common one in the world's religions, and perhaps it should be dealt with first. The place where the gods are active is declared holy because of the connection they have with it. Thus there are sacred trees, shrines, stones, persons, beasts, and birds. The Jewish Scriptures describe s their sacred places, persons, or objects, among others: Mt. Sinai, the ark of the covenant, the mercy seat (or propitiatory), the person of the high priest, the person of the king. It is possible to sin through touching them (in the case of objects), or laying violent hands on them (in the case of human beings), all because they somehow stand for the Holy One of Israel. A gulf is fixed between him in his unique godliness—at once both terror-inspiring and attracting—and all that is not he.

The bridge over this chasm between the sacred and the profane is the profane become sacred: always by divine-human designation and frequently by a rite such as anointing. To touch such a person or object thoughtlessly is to sin. The offense is against the Lord himself. It can be "sinful" even when it is unrelated to any intent of wrongdoing. The divine power has passed to whatever acts as the "sign" (*'oth*) of the divine Being, be it person or thing. That is enough to constitute it sacro-sanct. Any unconscious contact with something thus made sacred is a profanation, an offense.

As time passed in Israel, the elements of animism and magic that were at the root of this notion receded. In their place came the idea of conscious disregard of the claims of the holy (Jesus, for example, "would not allow anyone to carry a vessel through the temple" (Mark 11:16), a sentiment testified to by the later prohibition of the Talmud against entering the Temple area carelessly clothed or using it as a shortcut). This was part of the intensified notion of personal responsibility that came with the period of the prophets—the eighth to the sixth centuries before Christ. Jesus was interested in people's sins, but Paul was more interested in sin itself. By this he meant a personification of the spirit of evil in the human heart. He set against it grace or the justice that works through faith. Yet Paul too was a great protagonist of personal responsibility.

It is sometimes erroneously said that the biblical ethos was exclusively social in its orientation at the beginning, that peoplehood in Israel was the sole norm for determining the rightness or wrongness of human acts. In fact, a heightened awareness of individual responsibility and hence of culpability did come with the writings of the eighty-century prophets. Nonetheless, the idea of personal responsibility was by no means absent in the earlier biblical writings. The concepts of right- and wrongdoing, praise and blame, always must be conceived in terms of the individual or society in the measure that these two are mutually related.

What is important to recall is the social nature of an ethical decision in *any* culture. The idea that man is able to make choices absolutely "on his own," that is, as an individual who is not dependent on other persons or institutions in his decision-making, in one confined to the modern West. Even there it is an illusion, but the increasing isolation of individuals contributes heavily to the idea that responsibility for a person's actions is, under all aspects, his alone. The authentic biblical idea, despite fluctuations of emphasis owing to cultural changes, is that each man is capable of sin in his own heart, but that this will be more or less true as the people Israel is faithful to or departs from the terms of its covenant with its Lord.

In ancient times, the possibility of the morally right

behavior of the "little man" depended in good part on the conduct of his priests, his sages, his kings. The same is true today. There is such a thing as a nation's morality. It is related directly to the conduct of its lawmakers, educators, churchmen, scholars, advertisers, and managers of money. The Bible never allows us to forget how closely the idea of personal behavior is connected with the *mores* of the whole group, starting with the human family.

A thing is right or wrong for an individual precisely because of its effect on others. Setting up human nature as the proximate norm of morality and then understanding by "nature" the nature of the isolated individual does violence to the only kind of human being there is: the individual in society. God places no hopes in his creature man—man his son, his daughter—that cannot be fulfilled in the group. In this sense all morality—and in a special way because of the concept of the church Christian morality—is relative. People discover what is right for them to do as individuals before God only in terms of their relation to their fellowmen, in certain cases their fellow-baptized in the community of faith.

Reference was made above to the diminished scene of the sacred in Israel, which resulted in its becoming the property of a limited number of places, persons, and objects, all of them related by designation to the Lord. The notion of the unconscious offense or sin diminished in proportion. It never disappeared entirely. There are traces of it still in various Christian liturgies, where forgiveness is asked for sins of which the penitent may not be aware.

The latter phrase has the pious sound of complete contrition, but in fact it testifies to a time in the life of the church when there was still belief in the disturbance of cosmic harmony by the contravention of

33

some tabu. Quite unconsciously, one had failed to make a reverence in a sacred shrine, had spoken a word at which scandal was taken, had failed to purify a ciborium sufficiently, and the mischief was done. This object-morality based on impersonal "I-it" considerations, in contrast to the "I-Thou" relationship between persons and God and among persons, which came to be more explicitly proposed throughout the Bible, is unworthy of the Christian. Redemption in Jesus Christ means disclosure to the Christian, if it means anything, of the full measure of freedom one has to be a person before God.

Any reversion to impersonal offenses by means of totems or a disturbed balance in the universe is a denial of the relation of man to God that has been progressively revealed to us. The achievement of the biblical period—in both its phases—was that it removed men and things from God's place, thus permitting the possibility of adoring him alone. Symbolism of some sort will always be necessary to convey the reality of God. It may be the symbol of the cosmos, of human history, of the written word, of the Spirit-filled Jesus of Nazareth. Christ Jesus alone among men is deserving of divine honors because the fullness of the godhead dwells in him bodily (see Colossians 2:9). Everything else is a potential threat to the unique majesty of God, for there is always the possibility that things will be put in his place: symbol for Reality, creature for Creator.

It is sometimes erroneously said that the biblical ethos was exclusively social in its orientation at the beginning, that peoplehood in Israel was the sole norm for determining the rightness or wrongness of human acts. In fact, a heightened awareness of individual responsibility and hence of culpability did come with the writings of the eighty-century prophets. Nonetheless,

34

the idea of personal responsibility was by no means absent in the earlier biblical writings. The concepts of right- and wrongdoing, praise and blame, always must be conceived in terms of the individual or society in the measure that these two are mutually related.

What is important to recall is the social nature of an ethical decision in *any* culture. The idea that man is able to make choices absolutely "on his own," that is, as an individual who is not dependent on other persons or institutions in his decision-making, in one confined to the modern West. Even there it is an illusion, but the increasing isolation of individuals contributes heavily to the idea that responsibility for a person's actions is, under all aspects, his alone. The authentic biblical idea, despite fluctuations of emphasis owing to cultural changes, is that each man is capable of sin in his own heart, but that this will be more or less true as the people Israel is faithful to or departs from the terms of its covenant with its Lord.

In ancient times, the possibility of the morally right behavior of the "little man" depended in good part on the conduct of his priests, his sages, his kings. The same is true today. There is such a thing as a nation's morality. It is related directly to the conduct of its lawmakers, educators, churchmen, scholars, advertisers, and managers of money. The Bible never allows us to forget how closely the idea of personal behavior is connected with the *mores* of the whole group, starting with the human family.

A thing is right or wrong for an individual precisely because of its effect on others. Setting up human nature as the proximate norm of morality and then understanding by "nature" the nature of the isolated individual does violence to the only kind of human being there is: the individual in society. God places no hopes in his creature man—man his son, his daughter—that cannot be fulfilled in the group. In this sense all morality—and in a special way because of the concept of the church Christian morality—is relative. People discover what is right for them to do as individuals before God only in terms of their relation to their fellowmen, in certain cases their fellow-baptized in the community of faith.

Reference was made above to the diminished scene of the sacred in Israel, which resulted in its becoming the property of a limited number of places, persons, and objects, all of them related by designation to the Lord. The notion of the unconscious offense or sin diminished in proportion. It never disappeared entirely. There are traces of it still in various Christian liturgies, where forgiveness is asked for sins of which the penitent may not be aware.

The latter phrase has the pious sound of complete contrition, but in fact it testifies to a time in the life of the church when there was still belief in the disturbance of cosmic harmony by the contravention of some tabu. Quite unconsciously, one had failed to make a reverence in a sacred shrine, had spoken a word at which scandal was taken, had failed to purify a ciborium sufficiently, and the mischief was done. This object-morality based on impersonal "I-it" considerations, in contrast to the "I-Thou" relationship between persons and God and among persons, which came to be more explicitly proposed throughout the Bible, is unworthy of the Christian. Redemption in Jesus Christ means disclosure to the Christian, if it means anything, of the full measure of freedom one has to be a person before God.

Any reversion to impersonal offenses by means of totems or a disturbed balance in the universe is a denial of the relation of man to God that has been progressively revealed to us. The achievement of the biblical period—in both its phases—was that it removed men and things from God's place, thus permitting the possibility of adoring him alone. Symbolism of some sort will always be necessary to convey the reality of God. It may be the symbol of the cosmos, of human history, of the written word, of the Spirit-filled Jesus of Nazareth. Christ Jesus alone among men is deserving of divine honors because the fullness of the godhead dwells in him bodily (see Colossians 2:9). Everything else is a potential threat to the unique majesty of God, for there is always the possibility that things will be put in his place: symbol for Reality, creature for Creator.

The apostheosizing of sacred signs is, in a sense, the one offense that Christian morality cannot abide. Yet we Christians commit it all the time. Why? Because we will not let the biblical books in their full development speak to us. They tell us that the great sin against God is idolatry, yet that is the one thing we in the church cling to above all others. In the Old Testament period, men put their trust in horses and chariots and political alliances, not in the Lord. In the New Testament St. Paul mistrusts pagan sensuality, Jewish legalism, and gentile philosophy, all for the same reason. They manifest a confidence in "the flesh"; they represent a falling away from God and a turning to the creature. In our day, we tend to trust in Catholic-schools education, in the church as a power structure committed to preserving the old order, in persons and offices in the church, in forms and conventions, as if they had some power to save. The Bible is abundantly clear, however, that in themselves they have no such power.

This recording of the chief lapse in Christian morality is important because we have let the convention grow in our midst that ancient Israel was an offender in a way her offspring the church is not. The Hebrews of old were "hard-hearted" in the Christian account of things (the phrase is biblical), whereas with Jesus Christ there came for the first time forgiveness, mercy, and peace. In another Christian caricature, the people of the Mosaic covenant sought salvation by the rigorous observance of the law, whereas with the advent of Jesus there burst on the world the new conception of charity or love. Before the Savior's lifetime, supposedly, only overt behavior was reckoned consequential before God, whereas with Jesus there came concern for inner motivation and choice. In a word, the Christian tends to think of his biblical predecessor and Jewish contemporary as someone deprived of the action of God's Spirit, having to make do with a sin-identifier known as "the Law." He views himself as the member of a new progeny that in Christ makes an about-face with regard to all the deeper matters of moral concern.

A careful reading of the whole Bible makes this position impossible to sustain. There we discover that progress is unquestionably made in moral sensitivity from the call of Abraham to the last years of the apostolic age. The life of Jesus is a very important milestone on this upward journey. In his person, he is normative for anyone who would become a son or daughter of the renewed covenant, that is to say, a person born of God in water and the Spirit. Still, the pattern of fidelity or moral goodness is already set by the time Jesus appears on the scene. Chapter 31 of Jeremiah (read in its entirety, not just verse 31 and the material surrounding it) describes the terms of covenant-renewal from God's side. Faithfulness to it from man's side will result in that Jewish reality, the pious poor.

Simoen and Anna, Joseph and Mary were in this

tradition. So were those whom Jesus praised for having read the law aright (Luke 10:25; see Mark 10:20). Ezra with his narrow nationalism had his thousands, but the prophets whom he never managed to supersede had their tens of thousands.

The pious poor who sought the Kingdom populated the ranks of the early Jerusalem church. They made up a good part of that Jewish community that, through circumstance, did not accept Jesus. The pious were those simple ones in both camps who knew instinctively that God was love, that he was above any law he might have promulgated to help man in his weakness, and that the essence of service lay not in observance but obedience to his demands achieved in the depths of the human heart. Man and women of faith existed, that is, in the measure that their religious leaders, either as legalistic rabbis, or the Judaizing party in the early church, or a juridically oriented Christian clergy, permitted them to exist.

Let us be quite clear on what this biblical morality we are praising consisted in. It was based on a great conception of God the just, the merciful, the forgiving, and a thorough-going respect for man and his possibilities. It was a way of human life at once submissive to God and independent, trustful of him yet self-sufficient. At first the guidelines for this way of life were couched in familiar ways: "Do this and you shall (literally) live; do not do that or you shall die." The precepts had ultimate seriousness with respect to human life, therefore they were a "command of the Lord." At no time did the Bible suppose that morality would be easy or that man was capable of it without the divine assistance. Israel's God is one who says, "I will be with you." For the Christian, he is none other than the Father of our Lord Jesus Christ. The promulgation on tablets of stone—how else keep a record for posterity in that age of baked clay?—and the open invitation to make a word-play on the malleability of "hearts of flesh" deceived none except those who wished to deceive themselves. From the beginnings of the covenant with Abraham, the invitation was to a life of maturity and fidelity.

What if sex practices and property rights and the price of human life were notably different in their expression then from now? Must the oak look like the acorn? The modern Christian is often put off by minor differences, thinking them the essence of morality. The desert chieftain in Israel may have had wives a-many, yet it was possible for him to remain chaste in his heart. The blood-letter could have let oceans spill for the glory of the God of Israel yet be a man of justice according to his lights. If he were just, then in some measure he was merciful. The wily Semite might be deceptive toward many, as a convention of his culture; but if the truth were in him, there were certain situations in which he could only speak the truth.

What is the precise goodness of biblical man, whether early or late? What makes the difference between biblical morality and any other? It is a way of human life based on the conviction that there is a God who is faithful to his word. To submit to him is to be free. To remove oneself from his active concern is to sin. He asks for reliance on him, but nothing craven. He leaves man free as he himself is free. He speaks through teachers—Moses, the prophets, his only Son—but he also speaks directly to hearts through his Spirit, the breath of his mouth.

DISCUSSION QUESTIONS

Do you think it would be a good idea to start more Jewish-Christian dialogue on pressing moral issues? What advantages might such an attempt bring to a local community? Are there Muslims to be found in your locality?

Do you think that many Catholics still have a "tabu" notion of morality? If so, in what areas of conduct particularly? Is such a notion easier to live with than the idea of sin as primarily unloving attitudes and actions?

How are the "I-it" and "I-Thou" appraoches to morality contrasted? How would you go about helping an adolescent to move from the first to the second?

What would you say are the most common forms of idolatry, in the sense defined in this chapter, among American Catholics today?

In view of the relationship between individual and social morality discussed in this chapter, would you say that a person is disqualified from holding high public office who has divorced and remarried? Would your conclusion be the same if such a person had a mistress, or a liaison with a man, and it was known to a few but not widely? If it was known widely?

Woe to you scribes and Pharisees, you frauds! You pay tithes on mint and herbs and seeds while neglecting the weightier matters of the law, justice and mercy and good faith. It is these you should have practiced, without neglecting the others.

Blind guides! You strain out the gnat and swallow the camel!

Matthew 23:23f.

CHAPTER 4

Core of Christian Morality

You have heard the commandment, "An eye for an eye, a tooth for a tooth."

But what I say to you is: offer no resistance to injury. When a person strikes you on the right cheek, turn and offer him the other. If anyone wants to go to law over your shirt, hand him your coat as well. Should anyone press you into service for one mile, go with him two miles. Give to the man who begs from you. Do not turn your back on the borrower.

You have heard the commandment, "You shall love your countryman but hate your enemy." My command to you is: love your enemies, pray for your persecutors. This will prove that you are sons of your heavenly Father, for his sun rises on the bad and the good, he rains on the just and the unjust. If you love those who love you, what merit is there in that? Do not tax collectors do as much? And if you greet your brothers only, what is so praise-worthy about that? Do not pagans do as much? In a word, you must be perfect as your heavenly Father is perfect.

Matthew 5:38-48

At this point, we need to specify the precise nature of the moral teaching of Jesus Christ, who for the Christian is "God's only son." It is this: In the spirit of the great prophets of Israel like Amos and Hosea, Isaiah and Jeremiah, Jesus demanded mercy rather than ritual sacrifice, a concern for human beings in preference to observance of religious customs (see Matthew 12:7; Mark 2:27). He wanted an openness to the demands of love and justice (often they are the same) in each situation as it came along. Jesus was an observant Jew, not a despiser of the law (see Matthew 5:17-20). But he claimed to know the spirit of that law because he had God's Spirit. He was also clear that in cases of conflict the letter had to yield to the spirit.

After Jesus left his friends, their teacher of what was true was to be the Holy Spirit whom the Father would send in his name (see John 14:23; 16:13). So long as Jesus was with his disciples, he was their teacher. The role, however, later passed to this Counselor. As church life developed, prophets, bishops, and teachers were among those cast in the didactic role. The understanding from the beginning was that all are to be subordinate for all time to come to the one Teacher in the church. This personal Spirit is not a code to conform to or an oracle from whose decisions there is no appeal. He is someone who helps people know what conduct is right if they will call on him, and he helps them do what is right if they feel unequal to the task. The initial convictions of Christians about right behavior derive from the teaching of Jesus. From this teaching the Spirit never deviates.

Jesus' teaching about morality is simple, though it is by no means easy. He wants people to be holy— "perfect"—as their heavenly Father is holy. He would have them say what they mean and mean what they say: no lies, no slander, no detracting from

44

another's character. For Jesus, every sin is forgivable by God but "blaspheming against the Holy Spirit" (Mark 3:29). In context, he is speaking about calling what is palpably God's work Satan's work. We may deduce that, in general, declaring true false or false true under the cloak of religion constitutes for Jesus sin against the Holy Spirit. Such a perversion is forever unforgivable, he says. He levels no such sanction at lust, avarice, or pride. The one great move against God for the Christian is resistance to the truth for the sake of advancing the cause of "God" or "the church." We have the Master's word for this.

When it comes to what he considers virtuous, clearly his norm is respect for the other person. Do not gaze on a woman lustfully, he says (already you have made of her an object, a thing); be faithful to one wife (you have made her one person with you); forgive your enemies (if you do not, you fail to accept them as your Father does); relieve your brother in his need (God cares for him in his way; so must you in yours).

It is quite in order to reduce the moral teaching of Jesus to its basic component, namely the importance of every human being in the Father's sight. He never couches his morality in abstract terms, saying that such and such "befits human nature" or is "an ethical imperative" given our condition of mutual interdependence. When he tells us to do to others as we would have others do to us, he does not so much enunciate a universal principle as appeal to our individual sense of justice. Jesus' morality is eminently personal. It is even what is called nowadays existential. He invites all to experience the pain of life, and then, as a service of love, reduce that pain in the lives of others. In this lies a person's joy. Brotherly concern is the supreme consideration for Jesus. It and nothing else is a fitting sign of praise of the unseen heavenly Father.

45

Jesus has no trouble whatever admitting that there are universal commands. Do not murder, commit adultery, steal, give false evidence, defraud, dishonor father and mother—he grants them all (see Mark 10:19). But that is only the beginning of the moral question. When is the taking of a life murder, the sexual act adultery, the withholding of payment fraud? To answer difficult questions in particular cases, one cannot envision Jesus replying: "She was married, wasn't she?" or "It was his two million, wasn't it?" No, he would surely respond to every case in terms of the highest motivations he ever put forward. The supreme motivation he proposed was that of service to the other without counting the cost to self. *This is the core of Christian morality, understood to mean the moral teaching of Jesus Christ.* What you *can* do in your brother's behalf you *must* do. More than he asks. Before he asks it. Despite his condition, even his condition of avowed enmity to you. Go the other mile. Give him your coat as well as your shirt. Lend. Give. Forgive.

The New Testament word for this unselfish love is *agápē*. The practice of *agápē* considers one's "neighbor" to be everybody. Better, anybody. Loving without stint is a hard course to follow, not an easy one. This is so not simply because we tend to look after ourselves rather than others (though this is the chief reason love is hard), but because love imposes difficult choices. Conflicting claims are made on our love—they always have been, they always will be.

I love my country. Do I love it in all the wars it makes, all the laws it passes or fails to pass? Can I endure a lifetime of its civic failures as a nation, which are moral failures?

I love my steady boyfriend, my fiancé. He asks me to prove my love. I know he is faithful to me and in all

46

other circumstances chaste. He respects me. Yet he asks me to prove my love. If I yield will it really be that—a proof of love? For if it is, I will surely give the proof he asks. Yet Christian teaching is that to do so would be a failure of love in him or me—failure to love each other as we ought.

What would Jesus say in the first quandary or in the second? I know what most moral teachers I know would say. Are they the church, are they Jesus Christ when they say it is wrong to demonstrate against the government and right to fight, that it is wrong to acquiesce and right to "hold out" in proof of love?

The whole church has the problem of fidelity to Jesus Christ. The whole church and especially her bishops (the *magisterium*, as they call their teaching office) must be open to the teaching of the Holy Spirit. So must all other teaching offices in the church. The Spirit teaches that war is wrong but that an oppressed people can fight for liberty and justice. He teaches that marriage is the place for sex, and sex is an important part of marriage. Meanwhile, life teaches that passion and circumstance do not always make it easy for sex and marriage, liberty and peoplehood to go together. Yet the Spirit's teaching is right and must prevail.

Some moral problems are easier to solve than others. Swift, stern reprisal for a small offense is always wrong (though passion may in part excuse). Getting ahead through manipulating persons is likewise always sinful. Using public office for private gain—not necessarily monetary—is always an evil course of action because it is a betrayal. Failing to clothe and feed the destitute is always a sin against love—although the line gets wavy over which unenacted pieces of social legislation constitute that sin.

Jesus told stories to convey his ethical convictions (like that of the good Samaritan; that of the rich man and the beggar Lazarus). He spoke in pithy proverbs, all of which said in effect: "Do more." He told people in a thousand ways to stay open to each other as the correlative of openness to his Father. He promulgated no universal law but one: the law of love (see Mark 12:29-31). He would not settle particular cases when asked to (see Luke 12:13-14), turing the conversation instead to what lay at bottom so that the questioner could shoulder his own responsibility.

He loved, and loves, individuals dearly; yet in preaching the glad tidings of salvation, from which church and sacraments derive, he absolves no one from the burden of decision.

What would he have us do who say we mean to be his follower?

He would have us love. In each and every case of choice or decision, nothing else is required of us.

But love is a hard discipline; to love deeply one must love wisely. One must make choices based on wisdom. As one loves the more, the choices grow harder. Deciding for or against theft—presuming one is emotionally sound—is a bedrock kind of choice. Deciding how to love four women when one of them is one's wife, the second a vowed virgin, and the remaining two married to other men is not an easy matter. The greater the *agápē,* it seems, the greater the pain.

Again, a woman loves her husband and their children dearly. She wants to express that love toward both; but if she does so sexually to him, she has very good reason to suppose that after another childbirth she will somehow fail in love to him and to them. She is torn over the right choice—and torn because she loves, not because she fails to love. The day is past, if there ever was such a day, when teachers in the church could say exactly what love's demands are in every case like this. On simple lewdness, the Savior's voice is clear. On the right course of action in the use of sex in a particular marriage, it is by no means clear—though for a long time in the life of the church, in good faith, we thought it was. We presumed to speak with Jesus' voice without full examination of the data. More sober reflection lately has been teaching us that it is impossible to speak in Christ's name on this difficult question until more is known about married love and the dynamics of family life, about population growth, about food and housing and education and play.

The general lines of Christian behavior are firm enough. It is the particularities that are hard to discern. The believer reads the Scriptures first. They are a book of counsel. God is man's teacher there, through Christ his Son. The Holy Spirit is the guide of all, but in a special way, of those who read the Scriptures from the standpoint of the teacher's office (bishops at one level, theologians at another, insightful persons at a variety of others). The taught seek guidance from the teachers, who in turn can exercise their office rightly only if they consult those they teach. Throughout the process, we repeat, teachers and taught must consult the Holy Spirit.

A preliminary answer, then, to the question, "How do I know I'm doing right?" is "Ask the wise for counsel, primarily those few wise among the many who have teaching offices in the church. Pray. Then act—or repent."

Jesus Christ is God's wisdom in the flesh. The whole problem of Christian conscience is a matter of laying oneself open to the voice he speaks with in the church, the whole church, through the power of the Spirit.

DISCUSSION QUESTIONS

Could you give some concrete examples from the past or present of the sin of slandering the Holy Spirit as explained in this chapter?

Could a John Birch Society member and a civil-rights worker both maintain that they are acting in accordance with the core of Christian morality: respect for every human person? How would you go about evaluating these two points of view on the basis of this norm of universal respect?

If Catholics began to take more seriously the idea that love is the supreme norm of every human choice, would this not tend to foster subjectivity and sentimentalism?

In the light of this chapter, how might a group of a parish go to work to decide a problem of moral choice involving communal action?

Is it true in areas other than those involving one's personal relationships—e.g., in professional or civic life—that the more one loves, the harder the choices that face one become?

One of the scribes came up, and when he heard them arguing he realized how skillfully Jesus answered them. He decided to ask him, "Which is the first of all the commandments?" Jesus replied:
"This is the first:
'Hear, O Israel! The Lord our God is
  Lord alone!
Therefore you shall love the Lord your God
with all your heart,
with all your soul,
with all your mind,

and with all your strength.'
This is the second,
'You shall love your neighbor as yourself.'
There is no other commandment greater than these."
The scribe said to him: "Excellent, Teacher! You are
right in saying, 'He is the One, there is no other than
he.' Yes, 'to love him with all our heart, with all our
thoughts and with all our strength, and to love our
neighbor as ourselves' is worth more than any burnt
offering or sacrifice." Jesus approved the insight of
this answer and told him, "You are not far from the
reign of God."

Mark 12:28-34a

Set me as a seal on your heart,
  as a seal on your arm;
For stern as death is love,
  relentless as the nether world is
    devotion;
  its flames are a blazing fire.
Deep waters cannot quench love,
  nor floods sweep it away.
Were one to offer all he owns to
    purchase love,
  he would be roundly mocked.

Song of Songs 8:6B, 7

CHAPTER 5

Is There
a Natural Law?

The days are coming, says the Lord, when I will make a new covenant with the house of Israel and the house of Judah. It will not be like the covenant I made with their fathers the day I took them by the hand to lead them forth from the land of Egypt; for they broke my covenant, and I had to show myself their master, says the Lord. But this is the covenant which I will make with the house of Israel after those days, says the Lord. I will place my law within them, and write it upon their hearts; I will be their God, and they shall be my people. No longer will they have need to teach their friends and kinsmen how to know the Lord. All, from least to greatest, shall know me, says the Lord, for I will forgive their evildoing and remember their sin no more.

Thus says the Lord,
He who gives the sun to light the day,
  moon and stars to light the night;
Who stirs up the sea till its waves roar,
  whose name is Lord of hosts;
If ever these natural laws give way
  in spite of me, says the Lord,
Then shall the race of Israel cease
  as a nation before me forever.
  Thus says the Lord:
If the heavens on high can be measured,

or the foundations below the earth
be sounded,
Then will I cast off the whole race of
Israel
because of all they have done, says
the Lord.

Jeremiah 31:31-37

Much of the world that has heard of Jesus Christ and calls itself by his name finds it hard or impossible to live by the lofty standard of behavior he proposes. Love for God and for all humanity is Jesus' way of perfection. To accept his challenge is the work of a lifetime, as any thoughtful Christian knows. Much discouragement has resulted from the thoughtless assumption of preachers and teachers that full fidelity to the Gospel is an easy possibility in childhood or during any age of a person's subsequent life. If all life is a growing, a striving to achieve a never-quite-fulfilled potential, then Christian life—differing from ordinary life only in virtue of Jesus' stress on selflessness and the Spirit's inner guidance to a goal—is by definition a dynamic happening, something in process.

The supposition that one has the fullness of the Spirit at any time is a dangerous one for the Christian. (It should be needless to say that Christians do not believe that the Spirit of God is active in their hearts only and not in those of others.) Equally deceptive is the expectation that at any point in one's career one will act in the fullness of Christian love—the effect of perfect openness to the Spirit. That is not the way it is in life. Our progress is marked by as many steps backward as forward. We can be crushed by the burden of demand placed on us—usually by other human beings, but with God's sanction claimed for it—that we be perfect at any (indeed, every!) point in life. When Jesus says, "Be perfect as your heavenly Father is perfect," he does not impose the injunction as a burden. The adolescent just discovering his body with its latent procreative powers cannot be dealt with like a grown-up who has long lived with the mystery of control. Similarly, no one can be assumed at any time to have arrived at the absolute perfection of honor, truthfulness, or chastity. Like lofty peaks, those states of heart and mind take long in scaling.

Instant virtue is no virtue at all. What seems to be such is likely to be compounded of large doses of ignorance of the issues involved. One accepts Jesus' invitation only over the course of a lifetime. A person who attempts to be a Christian is much more like an arrow on its flight toward the mark than a shaft firmly fixed on the target. All our Christian goodness is an approximation, an approach—though we should be quite clear on what arriving "home" consists in.

We should like to speak in this chapter of the last question raised. What is the perfection of human life? How does the good person act? If Jesus' invitation is a call to continued service of one's brother in proof of love for the Father, if he constantly invites us to do more, we need to know what that service consists in so that we can do both it and more. We have to be clear on our reasons for acting as we do, otherwise there will be the danger of following our feelings and sentiments. Out of "love" and a desire to do "more," a person could twist the truth benignly to suit his convenience, dispatch the aged with a hypodermic needle, spread sexual favors around out of concern for the underprivileged, and in general act other than in a way that is commonly called ethical. *Agápe* run wild, in other words, can cause all kinds of mischief. Love needs reasons, good reasons, if it is to be exercised rightly and be lasting in its effect unto good.

The reasons for right conduct lie in the human person. If a thing is good for humanity, it is simply a good thing. This is not the same as saying "good for any one person." What we said was "good for humanity," meaning the run of people in general. We may, if we wish, push matters back a step to say that a thing is good because God, who is the author of human nature, wills it. But he wills things in regard to us only in the process of being the author of human nature. Whatever else he might desire for us, apart from his revelation, we have no way of knowing. Once he brought us into being as a human race, it was forever settled—in a general way, at least—how it would be right for us to act. He did not reveal to us, not even in his son Jesus, a course of action in specific moral dilemmas.

He made us reflective, and he made us free. Hence, anything that threatens a person's freedom or one's power to think for oneself is immoral. This is so because it attacks an individual in what defines personhood. A man needs food and a place to live; therefore any threat to his earning power, to his freedom to live where he wants is immoral. He needs to beget children and to raise them in dignity; therefore his right to inhabit a common dwelling with his wife must be protected, and the possibility that his children can be reared and educated well must be realized. Any oppression of women by men, whether sexual or economic or cultural, is immoral. The lie is immoral because life would be impossible if no one could trust anybody else. The curse is immoral because by it one person declares he would destroy another if he could. Polygamy is immoral because it is hard on a woman's heart, sodomy or lesbian activity because it keeps two from fulfilling their full personhood as men and women.

So it goes in any catalogue of sins and virtues that you draw up. Plundering the earth, exploiting it greedily, destroying its resources and its other creatures wantonly are immoral because earth is humanity's home. It is the creature man—the responsible center of values that enable him to be and to be more fully— who determines the rightness of things. He is a creature who was first set on the way of his own rightness by God. Each human being has a certain stable quality within, whereby he or she always tends to have the same needs and to react to situations in the same ways. We call this tendency to act consistently toward the fulfillment of personhood "human nature." Within a certain range, it is unchanging. Individuals are free, and in that sense they are unpredictable; but freedom operates within a spectrum of possibilities, and in that sense people are predictable.

To illustrate: There is no known society in which the liar-on-principle is held in honor and the truth-teller despised. To deceive the enemies of one's people may be thought virtuous, but to deceive everybody is not. Brutal murder for personal gain is nowhere praised (again, we except codes that permit, and even propose, the murder of enemies). Adulterous cheating is a vice no matter how many marriage partners are allowed (even though at certain feasts wife-sharing may be the custom where, in any event, more freedom is permitted to the male). A universal human sense reprobates treachery to tribe or nation, "treason" as it is generally called. It turns its back on blasphemy toward the gods or God. It has no good words to say for taking one's life (except in honorable circumstances), for addiction to drink or drugs (though ritual ecstasy induced by such means is commonplace), for cruelty to children, to the old, to the infirm. All this is to say that the common experience of the race is that there are certain patterns of acceptable behavior. We may therefore correctly assume that these are somehow rooted in humanity.

In this sense, there is a discernible law of man's nature or being. There is nothing wrong with calling it "natural law." In fact, there is a certain rightness in so designating it, if we understand it to mean the tendency, the movement, the dynamic thrust of human nature toward its perfection as human.

We have observed that man, whether the individual or the race, is a creature always in process. If any law describes (we hesitate to say "governs") his nature, it will be a fluid thing because humanity is fluid over the ages. An example or two should suffice. The random taking of life, we said above, is not acceptable behavior in any human society. Put briefly, murder is contrary to the natural law. Whether on the day the story of Cain was written or the last day the furnace-doors were closed at Auschwitz, it was a sin against God to kill because it was a sin against man. The Auschwitz victims were innocent; therefore we call the Nazi crime murder. Murder on a large scale we call genocide.

Yet certain moralities, archaic and primitive, have approved the mass destruction of enemy peoples. The Hitler action in the 1940's that revolted all humanity had its antecedents in 19-century programs in Russia, in the *herem* or mass destruction technique of the holy war (see Joshua 6:17; Judges 4:16), in the carnage of primitive tribesmen. We have made sufficient recent moral advance, in other words, to be revolted by the massacre of the innocent. We are not yet revolted, however, by reprisal raids against the innocent for the massacre of the innocent. And the slaughter of combatants does not by any means sufficiently outrage us to take steps to outlaw war.

As to the taking of human life in punishment for a crime (we set aside whether it is done to deter others or to punish the criminal), it continues. Justification for this practice was on the wane ten years ago. Now it is on the increase. Once, such capital punishment was defended by Christian moralists without a qualm. They even held that the natural law indicated its rightness (the murderer had "forfeited his right to life"). Now many are not so sure, while others are sure that the natural law indicates the moral monstrosity of capital punishment (saying that the premeditated killing of an individual by society is an unwarranted barbarism).

Has man remained the same in his nature over the ages? Yes and no. He is the being he always was, yet in his fluid state he is always capable of moral refinement or moral regression. The human race continually comes to know more about the possibilities of its humanity. As it improves, the natural law may be said to change. What humanity once could not have known about itself it now knows. What is known now, it is to be hoped, will yield to better self-knowledge in the future.

What is to be said about the control of births by contraception or abortion as something forbidden by natural law? The first thing to be said is that it is unwise to yoke the two as if, demonstrably, both are the same kind of offense against the natural law. Sex has as one of its potential effects the begetting of children, although this is by no means its only purpose. Hence it can be said that all attempts to frustrate conception or to destroy a conceived fetus, taken together, are against nature in *some* sense. Some would hold that, quite as unequivocally as the taking of innocent life, the preventing of conception and the destruction of fetal life are equally forbidden because they are inimical to humanity, not only as policy but in each instance of contraception or abortion. The natural law forbids contraception and abortion in every case without regard to circumstance, these ethicists hold.

Such authors are to be charged with careless thinking, however, in casting their net so wide in defense of human life. The law of nature as it applies to man may give indications with respect to contraception that are quite contrary to those that govern abortion. It can be shown that equally inimical to humanity as interference with the conception and birth of children is the coming into existence of children for whom the world is unprepared, and in particular for whom no family is prepared. Many Catholic bishops and moralists have concluded that in certain circumstances sex activity in marriage that precludes the possibility of conception may be engaged in. The principle was first established in the acceptance of the "rhythm" method for just cause. It was described as a natural means of birth regulation and it was distinguished from all artificial ones (i.e. those that interrupted nature rather than took advantage of its dormancy in infertile periods.) The question now concerns the legitimacy of other means than calculating nature's rhythm. Pope Paul's encyclical *Humanae Vitae* (July 25, 1968) holds that the natural law forbids each individual act of contraception. He is not widely supported in the Catholic theological community regarding this line of argument from natural law, although he receives widespread support for his overarching respect for life. His view is thought by many moralists to place an intolerable burden on parents of good will who wish to be thorughly responsible in their parenthood.

Catholic moral teachers earlier in this century widely held such a view as Pope Paul's, but new realities kept coming to the fore. They needed time to digest these properly, and they are still digesting them: sharply declining mortality rates and the resultant rise of live births, the starvation of populations, rising standards of living and of education, new psychological stresses on parents and especially on mothers in technological societies. More, Christians only recently have begun to outgrow a suspicion of sex that was no part of the Gospel but has accompanied it almost from the beginning. The love between husband and wife (meaning by "love" the ordinary, passionate kind) and parenthood have come into natural and easy conjunction for the first time in Roman Catholic history in the debates and documents of Vatican II. Sex as a good of marriage apart from childbearing begins to be admitted. For all of these reasons, there is a growing realization among Catholics that it is possible for papal teaching and the hierarchical magisterium to be mistaken about a particular concrete moral question, and that they have been so in this particular case.

There is no such widespread acceptance of the morality of abortion, as there is contraception in the Catholic community. It is much more firmly set against it as naturally inadmissable. There the natural law argument survives. It does so in a more thoughtful and nuanced way than by the argument that all fetal life in demonstrably human life, therefore each abortion is forbidden by natural law because it is "murder." A better expression of the reason why abortion is immoral is that it attacks the total process of life, cheapens its value, and coarsens people's moral sensibility by resorting to the decision to stamp out life rather than face the responsibilities connected with it. The next step is to see whether it is wrong in every case, including instances of rape.

Human nature, while basically unchanged, is at the

same time fluid, plastic. Through historical events, it undergoes change while staying the same in its root capacity. Through man's reflection on the Gospel and his faithfulness to it, he also undergoes change. Once one sees that man or woman is a creature on the way to perfection, both as a member of the race and individually, one understands that the concrete moral demands on humanity at one time may not be those of another. Neither will the demands at a certain stage of a particular person's progress, or a Christian's progress, be those of another stage. We are justified in looking forward to a time when the human race is so perfected morally that tolerance of war and of capital punishment is no longer needed. We anticipate equally a time when neither the selfish anti-life use of contraception and abortion nor the unequal sharing of the world's goods need be major considerations in determining Christian thinking and practice about the use of sex in marriage.

The chief enemy of a theory of natural law has been the figment of a human nature fixed in its own perfection, as it were before anyone lived on the earth. In this outlook—basically that of a Platonic philosopher, not a Christian—everything about God and man in mutual relation is foreknown and foreordained. Humanity is a static quantity, fixed. It learns nothing and forgets nothing. Each human life is but the realization of the form or essence of the creature man. What happens to the individual is that he fulfills this ideal or declines from it. God is conceived in much the same way, though more so by an infinity. He is not boundless, personal energy and will, as in the Bible. He is perfect thought. He is motionless in his completeness, as the norm for mobile man.

In such a conception, it is supposed that natural law can be called on to answer the question of what a person should do in any given circumstance. Thus, the spoken word must always conform to the thought. The worshipper must perform some acts of religion, preferably on a weekly cycle. The sperm must always find its way into the vagina. The state must have control over the lives of individual malefactors for the sake of good order. And so on. From the evident demands of the natural law in each case, there is no appeal. Any deviation comprises sin.

The concept of natural law has a bad press outside the Catholic church, probably because it is so little understood inside the Catholic church. As a philosophical doctrine, the church favors it insofar as it is true. As a way to express biblical truth about man, it can be helpful. It has been harmful as often as helpful, however, because the "man" of natural law frequently has not been the man known to the Bible or to human experience. Its man is Platonic man; and while Platonic man is an interesting creature, the earth is not his home nor time his natural element.

When we talk about "the natural law," then, we need to be sure what we mean. The term is satisfactory to describe what is good for man as a developing human in a developing human society, as indicated by the total experience of the human race, past and present. For the Jew and the Christian, this natural law is clarified further by what God says about man in the Bible, for those who have these Scriptures by their holy books. It is clarified for the rest of humanity by a variety of religious and ethical traditions at their best.

DISCUSSION QUESTIONS

To what degree does the legislation passed in the various countries of the world depend on the rights and needs—the human nature—of the inhabitants of those countries?

Is a religious group well advised to press for legislation in a country when it is convinced that the matter at issue is a good for all humanity (e.g., anti-divorce, anti-gambling, anti-abortion, anti-alcohol)?

What factors does a married couple need to take into consideration in deciding whether or not to have another child at a given time in their lives? To have no more children?

Many people believe that a guaranteed annual wage would tend to weaken the national "moral fiber" and would therefore be in some sense immoral. Discuss, on the basis of what has been said so far.

"You can't change human nature." Comment.

*Stay on in Ephesus, in order to warn certain people
there against teaching false doctrines and busying
themselves with interminable myths and genealogies,
which promote idle speculations rather than that training in faith which God requires.*

*What we were aiming at in this warning is the love
that springs from a pure heart, a good conscience, and
sincere faith. Some people have neglected these and
instead have turned to meaningless talk, wanting to be
teachers of the law but actually not understanding the
words they are using, much less the matters they discuss with such assurance.*

*We know that the law is good, provided one uses it
in the way law is supposed to be used—that is, with the
understanding that it is aimed, not at good men but at
the lawless and unruly, the irreligious and the sinful,
the wicked and the godless, men who kill their fathers
or mothers, murderers, fornicators, sexual perverts,
kidnapers, liars, perjurers, and those who in other
ways flout the sound teaching that pertains to the
glorious gospel of God—blessed be he—with which I
have been entrusted.*

*I thank Christ Jesus our Lord, who has
strengthened me, that he has made me his servant and
judged me faithful.*

1 Timothy 1:3b-12

CHAPTER 6

Code Versus Christian Morality

Then Jesus told the crowds and his disciples: "The scribes and the Pharisees have succeeded Moses as teachers; therefore, do everything and observe everything they tell you. But do not follow their example. Their words are bold but their deeds are few. They bind up heavy loads, hard to carry, to lay on other men's shoulders, while they themselves will not lift a finger to budge them. All their works are performed to be seen. They widen their phylacteries and wear huge tassels. They are fond of places of honor at banquets and the front seats in synagogues, of marks of respect in public and of being called 'Rabbi.' As to you, avoid the title 'Rabbi.' One among you is your teacher, the rest are learners. Do not call anyone on earth your father. Only one is your father, the One in heaven. Avoid being called teachers. Only one is your teacher, the Messiah. The greatest among you will be the one who serves the rest."

Matthew 23:1-11

The ten commandments given to Moses on Mt. Sinai, it has often been said, are but a specification of natural law under ten headings. If one understands the first three (in the Roman Catholic division, that is; in other catechetical schemes, the first two) to be a particularizing of man's need to worship God, the observation has a certain validity. Even so, the remaining seven do not summarize adequately all moral imperatives. In form, the decalogue is related to other ancient codes of behavior handed down unilaterally by sovereigns, of which Hammurabi's code of laws (18-century B.C. Babylon) is the best known. Clearly, no teaching about human conduct that purports to be from God can be anything but an explicitation of natural law. Worship behavior may be made specific, for example the Sabbath observance or the Eucharistic meal as an anticipatory and a remembrance rite of Jesus' presence. In the ethical realm, more strictly speaking, no principles or practices can be inculcated other than those that befit the creature man.

Thus, the letters of St. Paul and the so-called catholic (general) and pastoral epistles tend to list virtues and vices or give counsel to persons in various states of lie in a way one might expect from any lofty non-Christian moralist. The list of evil deeds a person can commit, found on Jesus' lips in Mark 7:21-22, is in this category.

St. Paul goes further in his epistles than listing things to be done and to be avoided. He proposes as the norm of all behavior life "in Christ." This phrase occurs more than 150 times in his writings and those of his associates. He means by it that the Christian's association with the Lord is to be so close that anything he does should conjure up the image of Christ's doing it in him. Sin by the Christian is for Paul a debasement of Christ. The baptized person lives in the Master and he in the baptized in such a way that Christ is the Christian's law (see Romans 8:2; Galatians 6:2). No external precept given through Moses or Jesus or anyone else is binding. The Christian acts according to a law written in the heart. Conformity to the spirit of

Christ in all matters is the means by which faithfulness to that inscription in the heart is achieved.

There is a special difficulty in St. Paul concerning a morality of law. Paul claimed to be a Pharisee; he had lived for so long by adherence to a code as the way of salvation that when he encountered Christ as a teacher who saves by faith he turned almost fiercely on the piety of his youth. In following Jesus, Paul was never far from the teaching of the prophets, and they at no time repudiated Moses' law. He set himself against the prevailing rabbinic teaching, however, which held that salvation lay in keeping faithfully all precepts large and small.

Paul's reaction had certain clear elements of "overkill." The law as an expression of God's will for men remained in force. Jesus had insisted on this. It was the law as talisman or guarantor of salvation that St. Paul attacked. He called it a stop-gap measure that had as its chief merit reminding us of the guilt we incurred through falling short of its demands. He said that in Christ we were free from the law—not just its prescriptions about pork and the Sabbath but the whole law. It is God's grace bestowed in Christ within us that makes us holy, not our efforts to bring our lives into line with a code promulgated from without.

The difficulty with the above statement of Paul's problem is this: If the decalogue is a specification of the law written in our beings, it cannot accurately be called something coming "from without." Similarly, if God was its author, as Paul believed, one cannot imagine this devout Jew attacking a divine deed. What he obviously was opposing was the claims of men to a way of holiness made sure of by their own efforts. A personal God had inaugurated an order of graciousness toward man in the beginning. It was he who was to be the chief actor in the drama of man's salvation.

He provided the law as a kindness. It was the best settlement he could get from the Israelites at the time. But this kindness—in the event, so badly misunderstood—did nothing to negate his promises made at the beginning of history that salvation would come through a personal deliverer.

For St. Paul, man's capacity for self-deception is boundless. Man says something like this: "I shall read the rule-book. I shall follow it to the letter. And I shall be saved. Nothing can go awry, so great will be my fidelity to what is written." But in God's plan, said Paul, no such slavish procedure was indicated. Man had only to wait for the fulfillment of God's promise. When this took place, it was in the person of a Jew born under the law. God's way of salvation was that free persons should answer the call of a supremely free God, conforming themselves to the person of his son. A personal Spirit would see to it that this always remained a possibility. There was to be nothing mechanistic about it. No word was said about impersonal compliance with standards. Persons would be confronted by the person of Christ; they would accept his call to be like him or would reject the call. He was the free creature *par excellence,* a man who was the perfect son of God. Thoughtful conformity to Christ became the whole law for the Christian.

The Jewish community, meantime, was doing something on its own to correct the abuses Paul thought he had observed in his young manhood. It was compiling a book of cases, the *Mishnah,* that did not relate closely to Scripture, and other books of homiletic commentaries that did, the *Midrashim.* These had as their purpose a regulation of the ethical lives of Jews in a spirit of perfect interior fidelity.

With all this said, a few matters should be coming clear.

There is such a thing as a natural law. It is embodied seminally in the Mosaic teaching, although the Sinai wanderers, like all humanity, were cultural captives of their time. Jesus could not wish us to reject any insights we might derive from reflection on our nature as human beings. That is to say, the Gospel (and after it the Talmud) cannot be at odds with the natural law. All are faithful readings of the meaning of man.

The Gospel, however, is not a philosophy. It has an ethic, but this ethic is not one that stems from the reflections of sages. It derives from the living voice of Jesus, a teacher of truth sent from God. Any recourse to thought-out philosophies of conduct as more dependable than his teaching is illegitimate for the Christian. Jesus knew that truth can speak with many voices, but he did not grant that any was superior to his as he spoke for God. The Christian will not shrink from a natural law ethic, therefore, provided it is not put in the place of the Gospel. At the same time, he will not abide impersonalism or code behavior as his sole morality, despite the legitimate insights it may provide him. He knows that he can settle his conscience best, both as an individual and as a member of society, by inquiring into what the basic teaching of Jesus indicates and applying it in particular cases.

We are left with two important questions. One is: Why has there been so much stress on the "law of God" and the "law of the church" if such an approach to morality does not have much Gospel sanction? The other is: How can a return be made in the moral lives of Catholics to a more authentic way? As to the first, the sad fact is that human nature always tends to seek assurances about life at a less than fully human level. From the day Moses came down from Sinai, and equally from the afternoon of Pentecost, people have attempted to make settlements with God at a level below that of personal responsibility. They have arrived at formulas of their own devising, and they claimed that this was what he told them to do. Jesus encountered this mentality with the doctors of the law. The Christian encounters it with some of the clergy and laity. "This do and thou shalt live," is the assurance sought. But Jesus taught the availability of life only on terms of repentance, faith, and personal engagement with God through him.

Conforming oneself completely to God's commands gives every appearance of being a dedicated service to him. What more could be asked in the way of personal commitment? The difficulty is that, given this mentality, his "commands" tend to expand by a kind of law in direct ratio to the need to be other-directed. Also, one can readily think that they provide the assurance that everything has been done that is required. The burden of constant individual decisions is consolidated under a few major decisions simplistically arrived at. In that way, one can never be faulted by God. The claim can always be made, in response to challenge, that one has fulfilled all justice. Whatever the heavenly ledgers may say, they *have* to record the unimpeachable deeds of the religiously observant man or woman.

But what seems to be submission to the personal will of God in the devotee of code morality is actually an attempt to bring God under the person's will. The terms are declared to be from heaven; the individual simply obeys. In fact, the terms were earth-born very early in the process. All kinds of observance of human devising are packaged together and labeled "the will of God." Openness to God as to someone interested in each personal decision is passed up as too frightening an option. Thus, the very essence of Jewish and of Christian morality can be overturned.

Another reason for the past and present stress in the

Christian world on God's address to the human heart as "law" is the twofold triumph of Hellenic harmony and Roman law. If the universe is ordered in all its parts, then human behavior is predictable in all its manifestations. A God of absolute freedom—not of caprice but of freedom—is the only God known to the Bible. A God of predictability in all matters human, the God of philosophy, is a real threat to the God of Job, to that Father to whom Jesus cried out from the cross with a loud cry. This God of philosophy tends to dislodge the God of revelation in the moral sphere. His will need not be sought from him in individual, anguished cases since it can always be learned by applying the pertinent principles. Personal freedom has little place in a Greek cosmos.

The Roman influence was of a different kind. The genius that brought the empire into being, built its roads, and codified its laws became a Christian heritage in the fourth century. It was only to be expected that legal settlements in the church's favor, like the adoption of Christianity as the official religion of the Roman Empire, would have their influence on the Gospel. The Emperor Gratian's code held that the Roman see was to be judged by no one. Justinian proposed the axiom that a king's will was the supreme law. This centralizing of power in favor of the Christian religion and making it explicit in a code of laws had its effect on Christian morality.

The harmony of the Greeks and the administrative genius of the Romans, together, made evangelical behavior a kind of fugitive. Rather, this behavior was recast in new guises that made it hard to identify as the teaching of Jesus. St. Augustine, who first put the ten commandments at the service of Christ's two, love of God and love of neighbor, insisted that only the Holy Spirit could bring music from this ten-stringed lyre.

The code was death-dealing apart from its interiorizing by the life-giving Spirit, he said. But history outwitted Augustine. Christian behavior as a morality of law can be dated, catechetically at least, to the contribution he never intended to make, namely that of teaching Christian life under the headings of the ten commandments. The blame, however, does not rest on Augustine. The tendency to slip away from the Spirit's influence into legalism seems endemic to the human condition. Certainly the Church has never been a stranger to it, in one way or another.

While a juridic or legalist approach to behavior is reprehensible, the notion that certain areas of conduct are divinely commanded or forbidden is not. Thus, one is hard pressed to name circumstances in which taking another man's wife from under his eyes would be virtuous conduct. The well-considered blasphemy, the selfish and premeditated sex activity of the unmarried, the careful attempt to damage another's reputation—in government parlance, to "destroy him"—are all of them inimical to human happiness. Quite simply, therefore, they are forbidden.

Still, the Christian does not abstain from these lines of conduct because of a universal prohibition only, divine though it may be. He examines to see how in each case the proposed course of action would be a sin against personal love. He may be deterred by superstition or fear of punishment. Yet neither motive is worthy of him as a Christian. They may initiate a process of thought; they may not conclude it. The law of God forbids things like slander, blasphemy, and lust, that much is true. How any of the three becomes a rupture of the bond of esteem for persons, oneself or another or others, is the question one must answer for oneself if the law of conduct is Christ. A beginning may be made with the knowledge of a prohibition and the fear of punishment. An end may not be made there. The Christian must ask: "How is this act, so attractive on the face of it, a choice against my neighbor or my own human nature, hence a choice against God? I have heard it described as a sin. Why, in this case, is it a refusal to love and for that reason a sin for me?"

Law codes are deeply ingrained in human practice, and they are not to be despised. Anglo-American common law, even though it comes into existence differently from code law, ends up as a powerful guide to human conduct by telling us what is "on the books."

This chapter is not taking a stand against either clarity or sanction in matters of behavior. It is saying only that Christian morality, though it may begin with a demand or a prohibition, goes much deeper to ask "Why?"

DISCUSSION QUESTIONS

In the light of what has been said so far, how would you advise an adolescent who wants to know "how far can I go before it's a sin" in sexual behavior?

Many of us were taught as children that it is "a sin" to omit one's morning or night prayers. Do you think it is sinful not to pray? If you don't teach children that omitting prayer is sinful, how will you get them to realize the need for prayer?

How would you teach the ten commandments to young people in terms of personal esteem and love?

Does Christian morality, as opposed to code morality, put too much burden on the ordinary person to be generally inculcated? Is it, in other words, unrealistic, and could this explain why kinder words should be said for code morality than are found in this book?

What do the Beatitudes have to say about Christian morality as contrasted with code morality?

If anyone is in Christ, he is a new creation. The old order has passed away; now all is new! All this has been done by God, who has reconciled us to himself through Christ and has given us the ministry of reconciliation. I mean that God, in Christ, was reconciling the world to himself, not counting men's transgressions against them, and that he has entrusted the message of reconciliation to us. This makes us ambassadors for Christ, God as it were appealing through us. We implore you, in Christ's name: be reconciled to God! For our sakes God made him who did not know sin, to be sin, so that in him we might become the very holiness of God.

2 Corinthians 5:17-21

CHAPTER 7

What is
Conscience?

*Therefore we must no longer pass judgment on one
another. Instead you should resolve to put no stumbling block or hindrance in your brother's way. I know
with certainty on the authority of the Lord Jesus that
nothing is unclean in itself; it is only when a man
thinks something unclean that it becomes so for him.
If, then, your brother feels remorse for the food he has
eaten, you have ceased to follow the rule of love. You
must not let the food you eat bring to ruin him for
whom Christ died; neither may you allow your
privilege to become an occasion for blasphemy. The
kingdom of God is not a matter of eating or drinking,
but of justice, peace, and the joy that is given by the
Holy Spirit. Whoever serves Christ in this way pleases
God and wins the esteem of men. Let us, then, make it
our aim to work for peace and to strengthen one
another.*

*Take care not to destroy God's work for the sake of
something to eat. True, all foods are clean; but it is
wrong for a man to eat when the food offends his
conscience. You would be acting nobly if you
abstained from eating meat, or drinking wine, or anything else that offers your brother an occasion for
stumbling or scandal, or that weakens him in any way.
Use the faith you have as your rule of life in the sight
of God. Happy the man whose conscience does not*

condemn what he has chosen to do! But if a man eats when his conscience has misgivings about eating, he is already condemned, because he is not acting in accordance with what he believes. Whatever does not accord with one's belief is sinful.

We who are strong in faith should be patient with the scruples of those whose faith is weak; we must not be selfish. Each should please his neighbor so as to do him good by building up his spirit.

Romans 14:13-23; 15:1-2

Impatient readers of this book may wonder when we are going to get down to business. "How *do* I know I'm doing right?" Page after page of fact and opinion, of biblical citation and Christian history, but as yet no real help.

We have spoken of Jesus as the Master, and the Holy Spirit as the interior Teacher of the Father's will. Something of the kind of creature man is has appeared in these pages. Considerable attention has been given to the origin and force of law, both within human nature and from another source, namely God speaking through Moses, His son Jesus, or the church. We still need to discuss how each of us should respond to the demands laid on us by personhood and by sonship of God in Jesus Christ.

If we as personal subjects feel no clear call to a life of goodness, or if we think we heard such a call in youth but are growing confused over its terms, we must look into the reasons for our deafness or confusion. Most readers of this book will be committed to following Jesus Christ. They are simply finding it hard to know what he wants of them in a variety of moral matters.

Is there such a thing as conscience? Our first answer

is, yes, it would seem so. Man is the only being who is reflective, who—standing apart from himself—can view himself as a personal center. He knows what he has done. By and large, he is aware of the consequences of his actions. This consciousness of selfhood in moral matters is called conscience. It is the memory of one's choices; it is facing their effects as one is aware of them. This process used to be described by the figure of speech, "The inner light of conscience," but such illumination doesn't come readily in difficult cases where much thought and struggle are required. We are probably unwise to use a facile phrase for a complex reality.

A "good conscience" is the absence of any recollection of wrong behavior unregretted or unrepented for. A twinge of "bad conscience" is the recall of a minor infraction, or the brief but fleeting recollection of a major one. To be in a "state of bad conscience" is to think one has done wrong and to know one has done nothing to repair the injury. A person may feel guilty whether, in fact, he or she should or not. The latter situation we call "false guilt."

This brings us immediately to the question of being wrong in one's self-estimate. A person can feel guilt-free when he or she has committed a serious wrong and guilt-laden when nothing wrong has been done. There is, in a word, the possibility of an erroneous conscience. Nor is conscience only retrospective. It is also available memory in the service of present moral judgment.

All moral responses are learned. Psychological research, at least, *tends* toward this conclusion. There is a capacity for right moral judgment in every newborn infant just as there is a capacity for speech or interpreting sight and sound. Whether this capacity will be developed, and if so how, is a question that depends entirely on upbringing. We do not hesitate to say that training in theft, murder, or sexual license would lead to the conviction that any one of the three is right behavior. The famous "boy raised in the forest" might have some second thoughts upon learning later how much his conduct was out of phase with society's; but whether he would entertain private thoughts about his own misconduct is extremely doubtful.

Jean-Jacques Rousseau wrote in his treatise on education, *Emile* (1762), that there dwells in the depths of our souls an active power, conscience, "not as a prejudice and not as an idea which we have had grafted on us by education and custom but as an evident, innate *a priori* of all moral ideas which has manifested itself in every history and everytime." If Rousseau meant by this sentiment (as he called it), which precedes all ideas or knowledge, the capacity for right judgment—or even a tendency toward right judgment—we cannot dispute him. Convictions in favor of right-doing that are geographically universal must be based on some inner human sense that is universal.

Still, a whole culture is clearly the agency that passes these convictions along. Societies teach outlooks, whether these societies be a tribe, a nation, a family, or a church. Individuals learn their value-schemes from the societies they are reared in. If they rebel in adulthood against immoral patterns inculcated in youth, such as selfishness or aggression, it cannot be claimed as a victory for innate conscience exclusively. Probably the adult comes on the more widely held view, the moral view, and opts for it as much because it is more widely held as because he innately senses its rightness. At the same time, there seems to exist the possibility of a conversion to truer or more refined norms of conduct in adulthood, e.g., the ancient or modern pagan becoming a Jew or Christian or

Muslim, a Hindu or a Buddhist, out of genuine preference for a higher way. We should not rule out here an "innate sense of the right"; but it is certain that the example of persons or societies is at work as the correlative of innate conscience.

We stress the strong influence of peers on the way we act because of the large body of experiment that suggests the acceptance of such a theory. It runs contrary to the view of Rousseau that a person has an *a priori* sense of right and wrong whereby, it is intimated, he or she will know what choices to make apart from the influences of education. It is on this basis that the "argument from conscience" is generally advanced and on this basis that any modern reader with a smidgin of psychological knowledge must reject it.

Like the case for natural law, however, the case for conscience is compelling if it is framed correctly. It does not attempt to say what an individual's situation would be if one were to be raised in a value-free culture. Actually, there are no such cultures. There has been but one "wolf boy" in history; therefor any hypothetical case put forward must be argued on the analogy of those who do not speak because they never heard speech.

The right case for conscience as an innate human capacity to judge is derived from the experience of the whole race. Exceptions may and do exist in every area of behavior; but in the main human beings act in one, general way with respect to values like the sanctity of life, the question of honor, the meaning of sex, and piety toward God or the gods. Wide latitude is to be found in each area. This does nothing to vitiate the principle that humanity in general knows that it is right to do good and wrong to do evil. Mankind's conscience—operating on each of us through the society in which we were reared—tells us that this is so. There is a "law written in men's hearts" and a "moral sense of which God is the author," but it is precisely that: a sense, a capacity, a predisposition to be educated in the way of refined human response to situations.

The conscience that *is* operative in individuals, then, is the educated conscience, the one that has been formed, or neglected, over a long period. Occasionally it has been malformed. Like any intellectual faculty—for that is what judgment is—conscience acquires a consistency through repeated use. It learns, grows, makes progress, or declines. The moral boor—say any ordinary street thug whose upbringing has been left to chance—is conscienceless in the sense that he is un-educated about right values. The answer to the question, "Wouldn't ordinary decency tell him that it was wrong to beat that old man?" is: "Nothing of the sort." All the influences that formed his conscience told him, "The weak are the easiest. You don't get caught because they can't fight or run." In the world of easy money, this reflection is the height of moral refinement.

Turning to the ordinary person, Christian or Jew or other, who has had better opportunities than the street thug, we see a person who consistently makes judgments on a twofold basis: 1-correct information on the moral character of an act, and 2-moral stamina (open-ness to grace, if you will) at any given point in life. The person needs to be clear above all on this: that it is important, indeed necessary, to follow conscience at its highest point of development. For if the teaching of Jesus is the supreme law of behavior from one point of view (this will both comprise the "will of God" and encompass any demands of the natural law), from another point of view the supreme law of behavior is the individual's educated conscience. This is because Christian morality is a dialogue between persons. The

Lord Jesus speaks, his friends answer. A human situation makes demands, the individual in society responds. The whole purpose of the dialogue is to make a person true to his or her best self. This is why, in the firstplace, the Lord Jesus addresses the individual.

All kinds of classroom arguments are carried on over whether conscience is the supreme norm of morality. The answer is "yes" if this means that people have no higher court to appeal to before acting. It is "no" if it means that man is superior to God or the community called church or fellowmen. No one, it is clear, can appeal beyond the highest awareness of the rightness of things that that person is capable of. Yet everyone can pursue a better awareness of what is right by appealing to the Father and Christ and the Spirit as life in the church reveals God's action in us. The whole church in whom the Spirit dwells can be a helpful guide in what is right. The time comes, however, when the individual himself must choose: not God in three persons nor the *magisterium* nor a confessor. At that point, a person's conscience (consciousness of rightdoing) is the last court of appeal.

Some of the forms taken by questions on the supremacy of conscience are these: "Has a person the obligation to leave the church if he feels in conscience he must?" "Can a once-married woman in good conscience marry again while her divorced husband lives?" "What of the suspended or excommunicated priest who says he knows in conscience he is not guilty as charged, hence means to continue celebrating Mass?"

The answer to all these hypothetical questions is the same: Yes, it is right to follow one's conscience; no other course will do. A presupposition of fact in favor of Christ's teaching against remarriage exists in the second case above, a presupposition of law against the priest in the third case. In the first case, the church-as-true-teacher no longer commands the obedience of one who leaves it. Such a person has taken his appeal to Christ, to God, or to the light of truth as he or she sees it.

In all such appeals to conscience, risk is involved. One needs to rely on God's grace and not on one's own strength. One needs to have exhausted the possibilities of wise counsel available. Above all, one needs to make a choice that is supremely loving of God and man, not a wilful choice to which the rationale of a "demand of conscience" is conveniently applied. People are responsible in all that they do, but they are not isolated or autonomous in all that they do. They cannot engage in any action without serious concern for its effect on the whole community of believers and on the entire race. At the same time, the believing community and human society often fail them, rendering the best choice theoretically possible to them one that is not open.

St. Paul is the first to employ the idea of conscience in the New Testament, where the word is *syneidēsis*. He is frequent in his use of it. Other writers who employ it, like the authors of the pastoral epistles that bear his name (two to Timothy and one to Titus) are concerned mainly to claim Pauline authority for what they write. St. Paul's commitment to the idea has in fact become normative for Christianity as a whole. The apostle does say that it has validity for non-Christians as a kind of law written in their hearts, since God never leaves men without some witness to himself. At the same time, the Christian's moral awareness (or conscience) is for Paul something that must be quickened by the Spirit, alert to its responsibilities before the judgment seat of Christ (see Romans 14:10; 2 Corinthians 5:10).

Paul is far from setting up conscience as an idol. It is not some internal moral governor based on a theory of harmony in the universe that makes God, Christ, or the church needless as the means of knowing what it is right to do. The assertion that "conscience must always be followed" finds New Testament sanction, provided that conscience is not taken as an independent, infallible guide, a sort of god in every man. The Christian community has never gone on the assumption that believers have no need of Bible, church, ministry, creeds, sacraments, worship, or devotion. Christian life is a whole. The moral sense of which God is undubitably the author, and all the formative elements listed above, work together to tell a person how to be "in Christ." Nowhere is it supposed by St. Paul or any teacher in the church that an individual would know a right course of action by being taught by God direct through conscience.

There is such a thing as conscience, then, and we must follow it. But we must be trying constantly to form our consciences by consulting the best guides available. What these guides are, and how we must make use of them, will be discussed in the next chapter.

DISCUSSION QUESTIONS

May a person always do what seems right, apart from the effects his or her actions may have on others? Why can one not feel free to do anything one wants so long as no one else is hurt?

How would you advise a person to go about forming conscience on the morality of modern warfare—in general or in relation to a particular war?

Do citizens have a moral duty to form their consciences on the issues of the day before they vote and to inform themselves on the records of the candidates as to these issues? Do most Catholics consider this a duty? If not, why not? What are practical difficulties?

Has a politician a right in conscience to make promises he knows he will not be able to keep in order to get into office and get something done to remedy existing evils?

"Everything today is so complicated that the ordinary person has to leave most decisions to experts about everything outside his immediate personal life." Discuss.

The Spirit too helps us in our weakness, for we do not know how to pray as we ought; but the Spirit himself makes intercession for us with groanings which cannot be expressed in speech. He who searches hearts knows what the Spirit means, for the Spirit intercedes for the saints as God himself wills.

We know that God makes all things work together for the good of those who have been called according to his decree. Those whom he foreknew he predestined to share the image of his Son, that the Son might be the first-born of many brothers. Those he predestined he likewise called; those he called he also justified; and those he justified he in turn glorified.

Romans 8:26-30

CHAPTER 8

Conscience and the Church

The Spirit distinctly says that in later times some will turn away from the faith and will heed deceitful spirits and things taught by demons through plausible liars—men with seared consciences who forbid marriage and require abstinence from foods which God created to be received with thanksgiving by believers who know the truth. Everything God created is good; nothing is to be rejected when it is received with thanksgiving, for it is made holy by God's word and by prayer.

If you put these instructions before the brotherhood you will be a good servant of Christ Jesus, reared in the words of faith and the sound doctrine you have faithfully followed. Have nothing to do with profane myths or old wives' tales. Train yourself for the life of piety, for while physical training is to some extent valuable, the discipline of religion is incalculably more so, with its promise of life here and hereafter.

Until I arrive, devote yourself to the reading of Scripture, to preaching and teaching. Do not neglect the gift you received when, as a result of prophecy, the presbyters laid their hands on you.

1 Timothy 4:1-8; 13-14

What guides are given us to form our consciences? A person who is not in touch with Christianity has his conscience and the wise men of his people to guide him—both of them gifts of God. The Christian has Christ as his teacher: through the Master's word in Scripture, through St. Paul's and others' reflections on it, and through the teaching of the church in the many ways employed by this ministering community. We insist again here that the Bible is the church's great book of moral doctrine. Her bishops and other teachers expound the truth they find in Scripture. If Scripture is silent on a specific moral question (as it is, for example, on Sunday worship, contraception, modern war, abortion, and specifics in the social order), the spirit of Christ must be diligently sought in each question. Here the practice of the church is a matter of no little consequence. If Sunday celebration of the Eucharist and the regulation of marriage by the church's ministers are ways of holiness the church has employed over many centuries, their force is assumed to be twofold: 1-that of some demonstrable connection with the teaching of Jesus, and 2-their status as expressions of fidelity to him long in use.

We should stop right here to discuss the binding force in conscience of a part of church law that derives from custom and not from the will of Christ. The laws of fast and abstinence and those touching Christian burial are cases in point. In such cases, the custom or practice has seemed good to some segment of the church (never the whole church under the same aspect, in any part of positive law that comes to mind) as a means of witnessing to the holiness of her Lord. Because she is a community of disciples, the church has never hesitated to propose courses of action—a "discipline"—for her members. She has, in other words, the power of legislating with respect to church life. No church law, of course, can gain ascendancy over the law of loving service of one's neighbor, nor that of avoiding scandalizing the weak.

The latter precept of Jesus is, in fact, the chief source of binding force for most church legislation. If by a kind of common consent a large portion of the church has a pious practice, disregard of the practice could well do harm to some who live at close range to the negligence. Whether it is carelessness about God's claims that is the reason for disregarding the practice or conviction that it does not bind in full force is, so far as scandal goes, not an important matter. The fact is that the neglect of certain precepts can cause spiritual harm to "little ones." Such are the persons who think that the church can determine by its disciplinary legislation who will be saved or lost, or that salvation is earned by rule-keeping. In thinking either, they are wrong. Still, they do not automatically lose their rights in the church because they are wrong (see 1 Corinthians 10:14-33). They are the church as much as any others, and they have a right within certain limits not to be scandalized. When church law has not yet caught up with the widespread practice of Catholics (e.g., between World War II and the late 1960s, when Catholic Europe had largely given up Friday abstinence), their scandal is spurious because it falls outside those limits.

Meanwhile, the whole church is doing these Christians a bad service if it fails to inform them about the actual relation between positive law and the power of the Gospel. All church law is an attempt to help people express their love for God and for neighbor. The celebration of the Eucharist on the Lord's day can keep charity vigorous. Doing without meat specifies penitential practice. Burying the dead with Christian rites is the expression of a faith-conviction, whether the dead person's or a family's. Each of these matters is a helpful specification of love, neither more nor less. Omission of observance on one occasion can be a sin against love, omission on a thousand occasions may not. It is up to the individual Christian to make a self-accusation of sin if there is any consciousness of guilt, whether the form the lovelessness took was spiritual sloth or the giving of scandal. The clergy and family members need to be careful not to press the claims of church law too hard, lest they multiply false guilt in those of delicate conscience and confuse themselves and everyone else on the true nature of Gospel morality.

One does not say of another's failure to comply with church law: "That is a sin." One has a way of knowing whether it was or not—and not simply because of ignorance of others' states of heart. The fact is that laws that "bind under pain of sin" do so and have always done so in a general way. Their effect can be cumulative, not in any mathematical sense but in such a way that, as one continues to miss Sunday Mass, one becomes increasingly unfamiliar with attempts to pray and to express thanksgiving. The right question to ask oneself is, "What did I mean by missing Mass last Sunday, by not having gone in a year?" or "What is clinging to my perfect record doing to my character? How long is it since I have lived by faith, perfect observant of the law that I am?" Since not all observants are by any means hypocritical or lacking in faith, the answer to the last question may be, "Does Not Apply."

Catholics have been badly confused over the way in which the view has been presented that laws of the church bind seriously, in a way that made the "binding" seem all-important. Such long-standing interpretations by theologians do not hamper the practice of Gospel morality necessarily, but in effect such has been the case. We who are a church of spirit have become a church of letter. We must take special pains to see that this shall not continue. All of our conduct has to be held up against the measuring-stick that is Christ, not one of human law promulgated in his name. His heavenly Father and he are the ones who help us know in the Spirit what conduct is sinful. The church tries to be helpful, not harmful, in this. Some of her sons and daughters have done harm in their attempts to help. As a whole church we must follow Christ and not them.

Pope Paul VI acted as a good teacher of law in his communication on fasting just before Ash Wednesday of 1965. He proposed that it be done on two days of Lent, Ash Wednesday and Good Friday, and then spoke of what the spirit of fasting and abstaining consists in. For rigorists who live by law, there was "nothing left" (although criticizing the Pope poses a practical difficulty for these people; he is supposed to be the chief magistrate!) There was nothing left, in fact, but the spirit of Christ, which the Holy Father represented admirably. His own Italian people have always had a relaxed attitude over the laws of the church. In this they are the teachers of Christendom. To be Christian in one's heart is, in fact, to be Christian. It is that simple.

Discussing the laws of the church may not be the best way to launch an inquiry into the church's role in helping us to settle our consciences. That is because there has long been a tendency within the Roman church—ever since the canonists of the 11th century, in fact—to be "solicitous" about positive precepts in a way our Lord spent much of his time opposing. Still, there is no safer guide than the church about Jesus' meaning on moral matters. By the church we mean the whole church: East and West, Roman communion and those from which it is tragically separated. The church has Jesus as its Lord. He has sent the Spirit of truth upon it to speak in his name. Even as Peter asked, "Lord, to whom shall we go?" so the Christian says to the church, "Lord, if not to you then to whom?"

Various emphases are to be found in the moral teaching proper to the different Christian bodies. Thus, Roman Catholics were traditionally distinguished by their concern for the rights and duties of individuals; but then came the social encyclicals of the popes beginning in the 1890's. The Protestant tradition in ethics is more on the side of social concern since the "social gospel" teaching associated with Troeltsch and Rauschenbusch; yet there was a long tradition before that of fundamentalist individualism. The morality of the Orthodox tends to be Spirit-directed, a Christian necessity too often disregarded; in practice, however, it can lead to a disregard of important social issues. The official teaching of the papacy and of Eastern and Western episcopates is important in moral matters; likewise the statements of the World Council of Churches and of the major Christian bodies. (The latter need not be "major" numerically. One thinks of the unremitting efforts of the Society of Friends for the cause of peace.) Through all these bands in the spectrum shines the full light of Christ. Seeking guidance through our Roman Catholic church alone is an appeal that we are not wise to make in any Christian matter, doctrinal or moral; but it is a good place to start.

Contrary testimony is sometimes given in the various Christian churches. In cases where there is clear contradiction (for example, the right to remarry after divorce), the Catholic follows the Catholic tradition as part of a faith-commitment to God through the Church that is claimed as a mother. When there is no opposition but a variation of stress (for example, the guidance available in one's country on peace and war), the Catholic should follow what seems the purer Christian tradition. In a painful question like birth regulation through contraceptive means, a question on which laity and clergy—including national bodies of bishops—are of several minds, obviously no single solution can be called "the mind of the church." Pope Paul calls his view that, in solidarity with his predecessors in the Roman bishopric. He wishes that it were the view of every married person, every bishop, and theologian; but it is not. All the married need to attend carefully to the lofty view of sexuality that the Pope is summoning them to. He is offering counsel that can bring happiness to many. Married partners must decide if their refusal to follow him is based on love or the lack of love.

The burden of decision on Catholics lies heavier here than in other matters. Situations like this, however, are inescapable. In every age, there will be some moral dilemma comparable to it: a relatively new problem caused by a sharp change in human circumstances, which the church has not yet been able to address itself to in any unified fashion. Early papal and episcopal utterances on the question, whatever it may be, in time will yield to new ones, even though at the moment it cannot be foreseen what these will be.

Again, certain cases of conscience are not easily settled by Christians of good will because the moral education they have received on them has been insufficient. Thus, it is widely recognized that in premarital sex many Catholic adolescents and young adults have arrived at the formula that intercourse comprises sin while nothing else does. They confess "passionate kissing" for the record, so to say; but when queried they will make the case that, in the event, "nothing happened." This mentality is the natural outgrowth of a morality of the overt act. Since the whole spirit of this morality is an attempt to name the point at which a materially sinful act took place, youth under pressure of the culture responds by dissociating all activity short of coitus from the category of moral fault. Having been taught the rules of the casuistic game, the young people proceed to outplay their teachers. They are incapable of asking the questions they should be asking themselves: How is this behavior, which is a sign of love, proving a false sign? How is it a sign of selfishness and not of love at all? How are we destroying love by "making love?"

The demands that should be put to the self uninterruptedly to resolve the question, "How do I know I'm doing right?" are, as a matter of fact, all in the realm of *agápē*. In every case, one needs to ask whether the requirements of love are being preserved. This inquiry is poles apart from sentimentalism. It is as objective a question as could be put. The object of concern is the motive of love or its absence. As to the act itself—be it abortion, accepting gifts in office, or expressing contempt for another—it too has an objective character. This may be described as the first determinant of morality, but not the last. Accepting sizable "gifts" while in public office is wrong. Was it wrong in this case? Mutual excitation by the unmarried tends to be sinful conduct. Was it sinful in this case?

This is the kind of "ethics of the situation" that the Christian is constantly engaged in whether he or she admits ir or not. Quite apart from the unfortunate connotations that attach to the terms "contextual" and "situation" ethics, such is the everyday reality. The concept does not deny objectivity to individual blameworthy acts. It tries to determine whether human behavior that is normally objectively wrong is wrong in this situation. There are some deeds so reprehensible that one does not hesitate to brand them "intrinsically evil," for example violating small children, failing to pay laborers, starving aged parents. It can be said unequivocally that they are evil acts. Short of a pathological condition, one does not envision a context that might reduce or eliminate their evil character. Wilful murder is in this category. So are lying to those one is set over and punishing the innocent.

To put certain sex behavior in this category seems an easy matter until one considers the unique force of the sex passion. It is easy to say (therefore we say it), that adultery is always wrong. Yet consider the difference between a married man's premeditated act of intercourse with another man's wife, and the normal conjugal life of a Catholic couple, one of whom was divorced many years before this marriage. Is the latter as well as the former to be called "adultery"? Would anyone reasonably expect the second couple to consider each act of intercourse "intrinsically evil"?

In connection with this question, many Catholic theologians in recent decades have more and more come to conclude that Jesus' teaching on divorce was directed toward those who are truly married, and much discussion has been taking place as to what "truly married" means. For example, must a given couple who were pressured by parents into marriage in their teens because the girl was pregnant necessarily be assumed to have given the free and informed consent that the church has traditionally considered essential to a true marriage? Must a marriage be thought of as a true marriage if it can be demonstrated that all interpersonal relationship has become impossible? In both of these cases, "subjective" as well as "objective" elements have to be taken into account.

All of us tend to rationalize our conduct constantly.

We deceive ourselves about the ethical character of our acts, put off moral decisions, lean on every behavioral crutch. The question is enormously complicated by physical addiction, as to drink, drugs, or stimulants. Sex behavior is joined closely to physiological habit. Deviousness and lying are habit-forming in another way. The human choice isolated from all considerations other than purely ethical ones seems so rare as to be non-existent. Yet no one is ever absolved from exploring the morality of all one's actions, a Christian least of all. A follower of Christ must probe, reflect, seek counsel, express sorrow, ask forgiveness of his sister or brother, and begin again. And again. And again.

A recapitulation in summary form might be of some help here. "How *do* I know I'm doing right?"

I know I'm doing right if I try to be pure in intention in all that I do—what Jesus called being "single-minded" (see Matthew 5:8).

I know I'm doing right if I consult the teaching of Jesus Christ, Lord of the church, in his own words in the New Testament, and Moses and the prophets whom Jesus relied on, and Paul and those other apostles who taught in Jesus' name.

I know I'm doing right when I consciously make my love for God through my concern for individuals (*this* man, *this* woman) the measuring-stick for every choice.

I know I'm doing right when I consult the church to help me resolve my conscience: its bishop-teachers, its theologians and religious thinkers, its holy and learned members of my own acquaintance. In all that I do, I mean to seek the counsel of the brotherhood of believers—and not theirs alone but that of any person of goodwill.

I know I'm doing right when I remain faithful to my conscience, which I have done everything in my power to inform.

I know I'm doing right if I follow with care current debate on the great contemporary moral issues heavy with social implications, on which the church has not been able to make a final judgment. I am the church, and my brothers and sisters need my help in this just as I need theirs.

I know I'm doing right if I pray for the grace of God in all that I do.

I know I'm doing right if I conceive sorrow for my sinfulness and not only for my sins. I must confess my serious sins humbly and sincerely, neither withholding them nor excusing them.

I know I'm doing right if I ask the Holy Spirit to make me a creature of love, a loving person in the human family and in the church: cleaving to what is right, rejecting what is wrong without fear or favor or human respect. What the Spirit *can* do in me to conform me to Christ as a child of the Father, *that* I ask that He *do* do.

DISCUSSION QUESTIONS

In a discussion on contraception, how would you distinguish between giving scandal to the persons present and helping them better understand the issues involved? Do you think such questions should be discussed freely in the Catholic press? What does the silence on moral issues in the correspondence columns of Catholic papers mean?

What are some of the practical consequences of attempts to be definite and precise in moral teaching? What are the possible effects of imprecision?

In what sense is Christian ethics a "situation ethics"? In what sense not?

Discuss, in reference to some of the moral decisions you have to make in daily life. St. Augustine's statement, "Love, and do what you will."

"If I fail to go,
the Paraclete will never come to you,
whereas if I go,
I will send him to you.
When he comes,
he will prove the world wrong
about sin,
about justice,
about condemnation . . .
I have much more to tell you,
but you cannot bear it now.

When he comes, however,
being the Spirit of truth
he will guide you to all truth.
He will not speak on his own,
but will speak only what he hears. . . .
All that the Father has belongs to me.
That is why I said that what he will
   announce to you
he will have from me."

John 16:7f.; 12f.; 15

"If your brother should commit some wrong against
you, go and point out his fault, but keep it between the
two of you. If he listens to you, you have won your
brother over. If he does not listen, summon another,
so that every case may stand on the word of two or
three witnesses. If he ignores them, refer it to the
church. If he ignores even the church, then treat him
as you would a Gentile or a tax collector."

Matthew 18:15-17

CHAPTER 9

The Modern
Moral Dilemma

*Some people imagine that morality measures our ac-
tions, not in the light of the just human ends which
they ought to be aiming at in the given circumstances,
but by a forest of abstract formulae which life must
copy like a book . . . In reality, the principles of morals are not theorems or idols: they are the supreme
rules governing a concrete activity the aim of which is
something to be done in certain definite circumstances, and governing it through more proximate
rules and above all through the rules, which are never
set down in advance, of the virtue of prudence . . .
They do not seek to devour human life; they are there
to build it up.* Jacques Maritain, *Humanisme Intégral.
Problèmes temporels et spirituels d'une nouvelle
Chrétienté.* Paris: Aubier, 1936, Pp. 221 f.

This has been a book about the formation of conscience in a context of Christian morality. It has not
been a book about human acts that are right and wrong
and that are taught by the church to be such (the bib-
liography at the end supplies such a helpful list of
books). When it has mentioned commanded and pro-
hibited patterns of conduct, it has done so only illus-
tratively of the main point, the formation of conscience.

Some readers are opposed in principle to a book like

the present one. They think that there are no special problems in recognizing right and wrong, hence that a book on the formation of conscience, however modest in size, is an elaboration of the obvious. They may even think it deceptive to discuss the formation of a right conscience because it gives the impression that there can be some question about how to act in specific situations. For such readers, the only books needed are those that spell out carefully the wrong of wrongdoing. Some readers content themselves with the fact that God or Jesus or the church has spoken against a certain thing. Others want further reasons stemming from the evil of the act itself.

A basic difference among people interested in morality (which, incidentally, connotes sex to large numbers while "ethics" connotes business) is that some approach the problem primarily from the standpoint of duty, others of love. Needless to say, love and duty exist for both—we are speaking of Christians for the moment, although all human beings are familiar with the two sets of values—but "duty" is the best word for some to describe their relationship with God, "love" the best word for others. This difference is closely tied to the concept one has of God from childhood: moral monitor, loving father, repressive father, tender mother *and* father, something of the stern parent and something of the lax, and so on.

The fact that Jesus taught human behavior by way of love, though he was no stranger to duty or command, is a sore trial to some Christians. They have been dealt a cruel hand by fate: a temperament or upbringing that inclines them in one direction and a religious teaching that takes them in another. Worse still, there has been for many what seems to them an unjust shift in their lifetime from a moral teaching of demand to one of delight, from the rigors of obedience

104

to the flabbiness of love. In fact, there was no such exclusive stress on obligation in anyone's catechetical youth, just as there was no exclusion of loving concern. There were tendencies or emphases, to be sure. Much more importantly, there was a whole fabric of home and family life determining for the young Catholic what he or she could hear when a variety of things was being said in the child's hearing.

The recent shift from obligation to love that Catholic teaching is widely accused of making has by no means created a single party of the disaffected. Perhaps as numerous as those betrayed in one way are those betrayed in another. They are the youthful rebels against repression with whom the church has just begun to catch up. Many of them write books and essays or sketch biting cartoons about growing up Catholic. In youth, they knew better than the follies that were going on around them; but now that the follies have largely stopped, they don't like it one bit. They have been unseated as critics. The permissive church that is now available to rebel against turns out to be not as serviceable a target of aggressions as the repressive one that at least had the good grace to look stupid. The rebel betrayed is every bit as sorry a figure as the conformist betrayed.

Another class of resisters are those whose thoughts have led them in the direction that says that since love understands everything it permits everything. That is a perversion of Jesus' teaching rather than a logical conclusion of it, but many part company with him over it. They speak of an "uptight" church whenever an attempt is made to teach in his spirit on certain questions. Thus, abortion is no one's business but that of the individual pregnant woman; lovers of the same sex have the same rights to public displays of affection and marriage as heterosexual lovers; all exercise of police power is brutal and repressive of human rights. These dogmas are expected to go unexamined, above all not challenged in the name of Christian morality.

The same Christ who has been manipulated by hardliners of one sort, in other words, is equally vulnerable to manipulation by hard-liners of another. A religious openness to the person of Jesus reveals, however, that he is not to be used in this way. He may be rejected, but he cannot be manipulated.

This discussion of types of response to Jesus' teaching puts its finger on an important matter regarding the attempt of this book. It is a treatise for the healthy. There is no special consideration given in its pages to what a former generation of moralists used to classify as "temperament, habit, and psychological state." In one sense, the mentally ill and the emotionally disturbed are the only persons unfree to choose. Yet in another, all of us lack freedom in some measure. Human liberty is a relative matter. The present writer goes on the assumption that we are free because we think we are, even though those psychological data are convincing that indicate that our range of genuinely free choices is narrow. Restricted or not, freedom is there. This is a position poles apart from the one that holds that the experience of freedom is illusory and not real.

Some people are freer in certain matters than they are in others. Compulsive behavior marks the psychotic, in a lesser degree the neurotic. It is not entirely absent, however, from healthier personalities. Compulsions are often unconscious in us. While they may remove culpability, they do not make ethical decisions easier for those who are ridden by them. If anything the decisions are harder for the compulsive. The essence of reaching maturity is arriving at a point where we make our ethical choices in a state of freedom.

Maturing is making progress from being unfree to being free.

Much of the earlier discussion in this book seemed to go on the supposition that people generally are free and simply need to learn how to use their freedom. Yet the present writer does not believe that that is the actual situation, and he wishes to say so very clearly. Most people in some measure are not free—for a variety of reasons rooted in infancy and childhood—and they need to learn how to be free. After that, they can choose. Before it, they cannot choose freely, and they must endure the excruciating pain of being told that they have to when in fact they are in no real condition to do so.

The implications of what has just been said are far-reaching. If very few in our society are totally free, very few professing Catholics will be free. The Gospel once taken to heart is a liberating force but only if it is taught as such; if it is presented as a burden, then the possibility of unlimited mischief exists. Jesus came to lift from people's backs heavy and insupportable burdens. An ill-considered morality or a doubtful doctrine propounded in his name can weigh them down unmercifully, especially those whose psyches already have been rendered delicate by a history of conflict or the threat of authority figures in childhood. The greatest injustice done in Christ's name has been making him a bully for the healthy when he came as a physician for the sick. The result is that he becomes a bully for the sick, the enemy of those who need him most. He came to restore to health and to teach freedom. He may not be represented fairly as an exactor of obedience or an enforcer of commandments.

Mental health is a billion-dollar enterprise in our time. The culture does not have a universal respect for its practitioners, but it has a nearly universal need of their services. The causes of emotional imbalance in the population are many, but high on the list comes a false censoriousness related to religion. Granted that many things precede it: discord in the home, parents preying on children, conflicting values within and outside the domestic circle. Still, standards that repress without liberating and that are put forward in the name of "religious" behavior are a massive offender. In any such scheme of perverse religious education, God and Jesus Christ become figures of fear and terror, not mercy and love. They are sometimes irrecoverable for a lifetime in their true guise because they have early been projected falsely with such great success.

The moral formation of the young, whether in relation to or apart from the claims of religion, has not been a concern of this book. Yet it has to be, if only by way of a strong disclaimer that a Christian conscience can be formed readily in adolescence or adulthood if one has been maimed by "religion" as an infant or a child. If that is the case, therapy may be needed. Repetition of the same moral demands and the same sanctions will not be helpful, however enlightened the phrasing. Readers who are genuinely emotionally disturbed over the question of morality can not be helped by what is bound to seem to them like more of the same. It is those only slightly scarred by their upbringings who may find these pages helpful. They need— and can be open to—a presentation of the Gospel for what it is: a liberating experience.

Most of the religious education in youth that matters for later life is received in the home, by what is said and done or left unsaid and undone. It is a commonplace for adults to say that they were distorted in childhood by the moral myths propounded by "priests and nuns." In fact, any child who has been well-formed by loving parents during the first four or five years is fairly impervious to inhibitory tales told by an outsider. It is the parent living in fear who does the initial damage, laying the child open to reinforcement by others who live in a similar condition of fear. One can ask, of course, what is cause and what is effect, the clerical or the lay outlook on moral questions among Catholics. No ready answer is forthcoming, nor is one needed. The burden of confusion is jointly borne, with perhaps the heavier responsibility on the teachers—clergy or clergy-formed. But it is a caricature to lay blame at certain doorsteps only. A repressive clergy and sisterhood could not flourish for long unless their services were welcomed by parents as external censors and monitors.

That, in part, is why the religion teacher of the 1970s is held in such low esteem on the home front. Not all are geniuses of pedagogy or theology, but they are in general an educated, earnest, and enlightened group trying to help the young discover their liberty in Christ. If they are building on an endowment that was first given in the home, there is no problem. If, however, they are apostles of true liberty dealing with a youth sent off to them for repressive purposes, after a childhood that conveyed a false liberty "freedom" only to obey commands—they cannot satisfy. They simply are not meeting the terms. Some may be fools and not wise in Christ. Of these one hears only rarely; whereas of the earnest and the enlightened one hears often. We speak of the 1970s.

We have touched above on some of the reasons why it is impossible to give any segment of the church, including its parents and its bishops, an absolutely clean bill as teachers of Christian morality. All of us are influenced by our upbringing and our present circumstances. The emergence toward moral maturity is not assured in any particular sex or age group or class.

There is, of course, the New Testament era promise of the Spirit to teachers in Jesus' name. In general, the gift is received and acted upon. But only in general. There are special handicaps to being an unmarried male of middle age or more who was charged in youth with the moralists function. The present writer is in that category, hence he can testify as an expert. He does not trust himself, any more than he trusts men of his own age and condition as a class, the more so as they happen to be less learned than he.

He does trust the whole church—the body, after all, to which the gift of the Spirit is given. That church has a rich experience. It also has a record of pusillanimity like that of Peter during the Passion. The Roman communion has been through four centuries of challenge from Proestantism in the West, much of it salutary, to which it has reacted like any body under siege. There has been a century and more of special challenge in which exploding human knowledge has threatened the foundations of those edifices of symbol, which all religions are in their deepest reality. This challenge is superhuman. It cannot be met by reliance on unaided humanity ("flesh," as the Bible calls it). It can be faced only by men and women of goodwill acting in concert.

The special ethical questions with which our decade is wrestling are well-known. They cannot be listed in any order of importance because each one touches on human life and dignity on a vast scale. They include the right of all peoples to freedom from oppression by other peoples; the problem of nourishment for all when economic patterns on the globe provide the built-in certitude that all will not be fed; the dominance of women by men, both in societies where a consciousness of this gross injustice has been arrived at and where it has not; the use of sex as a manipulatory device when it is meant to be an enlargement of the human spirit; the ethic of power in which all lies, deceits, and destructions are allowable in the interests of the economic growth of the powerful. Each of these problems is so huge that only political action can cope with it. Yet the church is not the state, and it can only hope that the convictions of its members in favor of human life are voiced in the ordinary ways in the processes of the state. They are the ballot box, parliaments, the classroom and other channels of learning, the media, and public sentiment clearly expressed. Obviously, however, the greatest sufferers are the disenfranchised who have no recourse to these means.

A common temptation of the clergy is to enter directly into political process, claiming that the mandate from God to teach what is a good for all requires this. This direct engagement in the lives of nations will never be popular, basically, because it accords so poorly with the spirit of Jesus Christ. Our Lord appealed to minds and hearts with a view to inner conversion. He cannot be imagined as having his supporters bring pressure to bear on the Roman empire or the Temple priesthood as a means to improve the human lot. If they acted on their own religious convictions to achieve the onset of God's reign in hearts, well and good. But entering deeply into the politics of a nation through a particular party or dictatorship—claiming all the while that morality, not politics, is the church's sole concern—is an unevangelical mode of procedure.

The teachers in the church have task enough in reaching believers. Whenever they take shortcuts and enlist the aid of Caesar (the "secular arm" of medieval theory), they are likely to grow derelict in their duty of preaching the Gospel to the baptized. It is because of the suspicion that they have failed in this duty and have turned to influencing public policy directly, after

111

that failure, that populations tend to reject their overtures. In serious ethical questions like divorce, abortion, and enforced sterilization, a strong case can be made for the presence of moral evil from which a variety of social evils flow. The people to whom that case must be made by a church is its communicants. The evil involved may be held to be such for all humanity, not just the members of a faith group. Yet only the members of a faith group can be expected to receive the teaching as a matter that is related to religious faith.

This does not mean that gifted religious teachers—individual clergy, rabbis, national hierarchies—may not take on the mantle of public moralists. But they will be effective only if they have first given proof of addressing themselves to their co-religionists, over a long period, on the basis of common religious understandings. If the populace at large suspects that there are no such widespread common understandings (i.e., as between religious teachers and those they teach), they naturally will resent an appeal to their consciences or, more usually, their political institutions. They figure that if clergymen can't convince their own, they had better not try going to work on anyone else.

There are some very important ethical questions abroad these days, like the civil rights of the homosexually oriented, amnesty for those who would not fight or for those in government who perjured themselves to escape jail, the crackdown on little drug offenders while no large sums are being spent to catch the big ones. The whole moral fabric of the nation is weakened by a tone of permissiveness by public officials who preach against it and practice it massively.

In this situation, selective indignation by those who presume to teach in Christ's name has no place. They must be compassionate as he was, but they must be absolutely consistent about what the law of God does and does not allow. They cannot be rigorous in sex but soft on armaments, press hard for a minimum wage for domestics and field workers but be favorable to administrations that perpetrate the abuses they are deploring.

The church, in a word, can be of great help through its teachers when they teach—not, however, when the pulpits of the country are strangely silent on all moral questions but three or four; not when the diocesan press is sadly predictable in the matter of those questions it will and will not entertain; not when churchmen take their case to legislatures and courts because it seems they cannot convince their own people.

There is a remarkably good job waiting to be done by a teaching church in helping a believing church answer the question, "How do I know I'm doing right?" People really would like to know, despite certain evidence to the contrary. The confessional was a marvelous opportunity, frittered away by "confessions of devotion." So is the pulpit, the press, the classroom. But not if there's squeamishness about sex-education in schools, not if friendly and supportive words—and press photographs—continue to be forthcoming about venal politicians in the hope of favorable legislation, not if church people piously talk about "going overboard on the social order."

We cannot have it both ways as a church. If we ever seriously put ourselves the question, "How do I know I'm doing right?" we have to engage in a deep soul-search like the one outlined above, then wait for the answer.

When it comes, it is very likely to rearrange our lives.

If an unbeliever invites you to his table and you want to go, eat whatever is placed before you, without raising any question of conscience. But if someone should say to you, "This was offered in idol worship," do not eat it, both for the sake of the one who called attention to it and on account of the conscience issue—not your conscience but your neighbor's. You may ask, why should my liberty be restricted by another man's conscience? And why is it, if I partake thankfully, that I should be blamed for the food over which I give thanks?

The fact is that whether you eat or drink—whatever you do—you should do all for the glory of God. Give no offense to Jew or Greek or to the church of God, just as I try to please all in any way I can by seeking, not my own advantage, but that of the many, that they may be saved. Imitate me as I imitate Christ.

1 Corinthians 10:27-33

Bibliography

Böckle, Franz (ed.), *Moral Problems and Christian Personalism,* Volume 5 of *Concilium* (New York: Paulist Press, 1965). Splendid studies on the dynamic quality of morality, the history of natural law, pacifism, and the state of the birth control question at the time of publication.

_____ *War, Poverty and Freedom,* Volume 15 of *Concilium* (New York: Paulist Press, 1966). Besides the topics indicated by the title, there is a good essay by Alois Müller on authority and obedience in the church.

Curran, Charles E. *Christian Morality Today: The Renewal of Moral Theology* (Notre Dame, Indiana: Fides Publishers, 1966). Nine chapters on the relevance of modern moral theology, including two on conscience and free responsibility, three on marriage questions, and one on Sunday observance.

_____ *Contemporary Problems in Moral Theology* (Notre Dame, Indiana: Fides Publishers, 1970, paper).

_____ *New Perspectives in Moral Theology* (Notre Dame, Indiana: Fides Publishers, 1974).

Dodd, C.H., *Gospel and Law* (New York: Columbia University Press, 1951). A brief and important study of the Christian ethics of the New Testament with special reference to the ethical teaching of the Gospels and what comprises "the law of Christ."

Drinkwater, F.H., *Birth Control and Natural Law* (Baltimore: Helicon, 1965). The dean of English Catholic ethicists recalls a little history.

Evans, Illtud (ed.), *Light on the Natural Law* (Baltimore: Helicon, 1965). Five essays including two by lawyers and one by an anthropologist.

Fuchs, Joseph, *Natural Law* (New York: Sheed & Ward, 1965). A careful historical and theological study.

Häring, Bernard, *Christian Renewal in a Changing World* (New York: Desclee, 1964). One-volume summary of the author's larger *The Law of Christ*.

―――― Morality is for Persons (New York: Farrar, Straus & Giroux, 1971), Justification of morality by the good of persons in community and by the community of persons.

Monden, Louis, *Sin, Liberty and Law* (New York: Sheed & Ward, 1965). A Belgian theologian devotes almost half of his book to the question "Legal Ethics or Situation Ethics?", the remainder to freedom and determinism, and the mystique of sin. Combines the best of contemporary European thought with good confessional practice, valid anywhere.

116

Tillich, Paul, *Morality and Beyond* (New York: Harper & Row, 1963). Profound discussion of man's true nature, created by God, as the source from which our actions must spring. Tillich is unsympathetic to the concept of natural law (as are many contemporary Catholics), on the terms in which it has been put forward by Catholics.

Vann, Gerald, *Morals and Man* (London: Collins Fontana Books, 1950). Reprint of a 1937 book by the most humane of English-speaking Thomists.